PREFACE

Welcome to the fascinating world of 'Coloring Canine Companions'. This unique coloring book was created especially for dog-loving adults looking for a therapeutic and relaxing experience. Explore detailed art of various dog breeds.

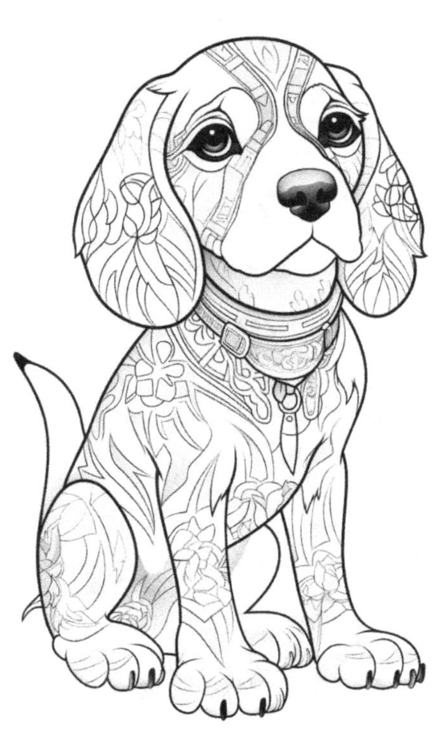

THIS BOOK BELONGS TO:

____

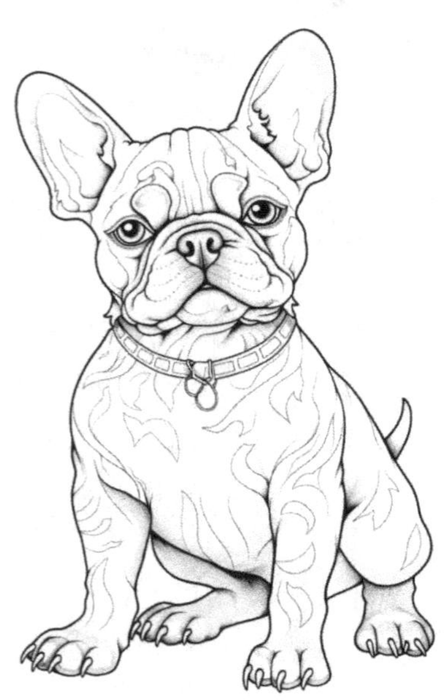

Test Color Page

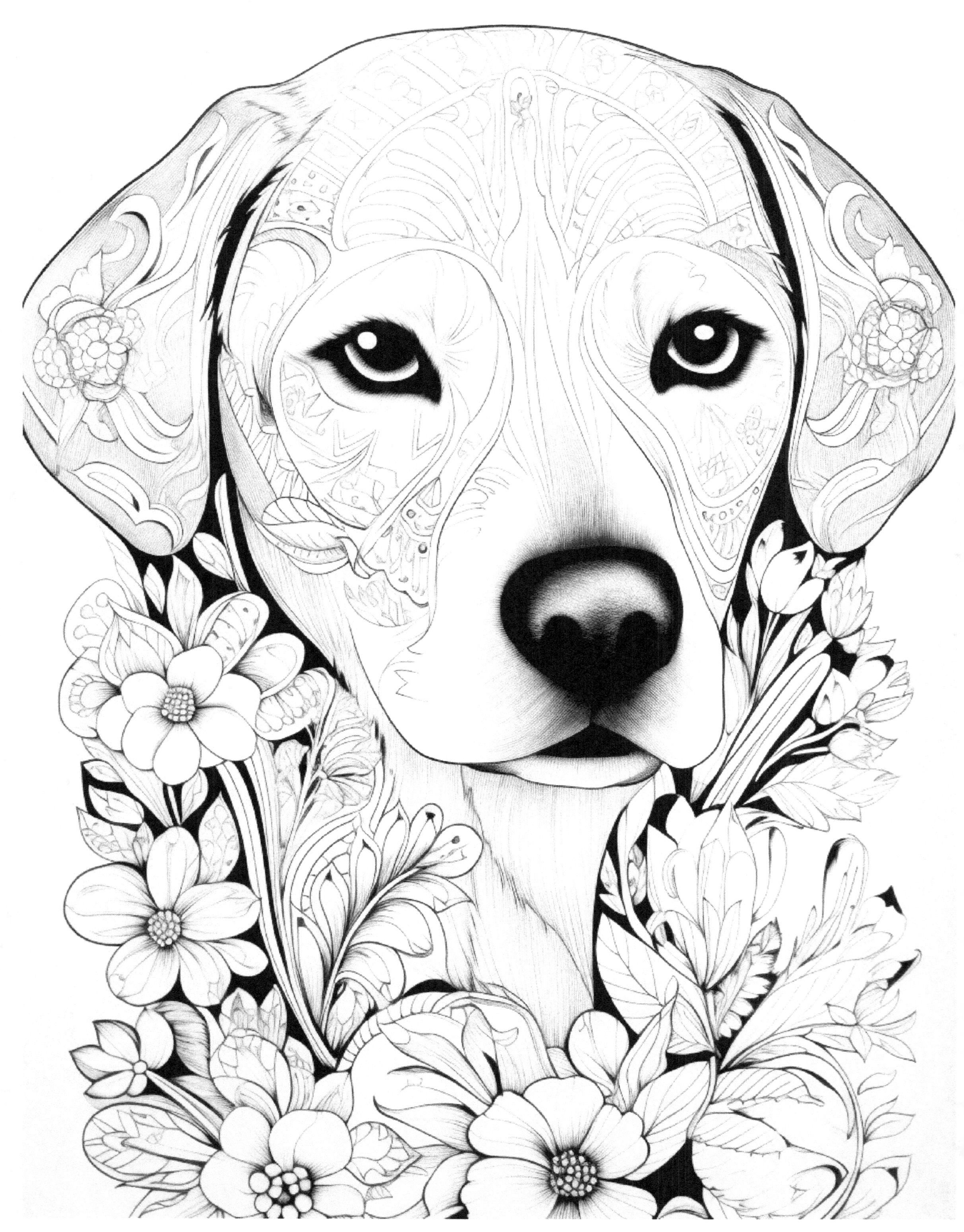

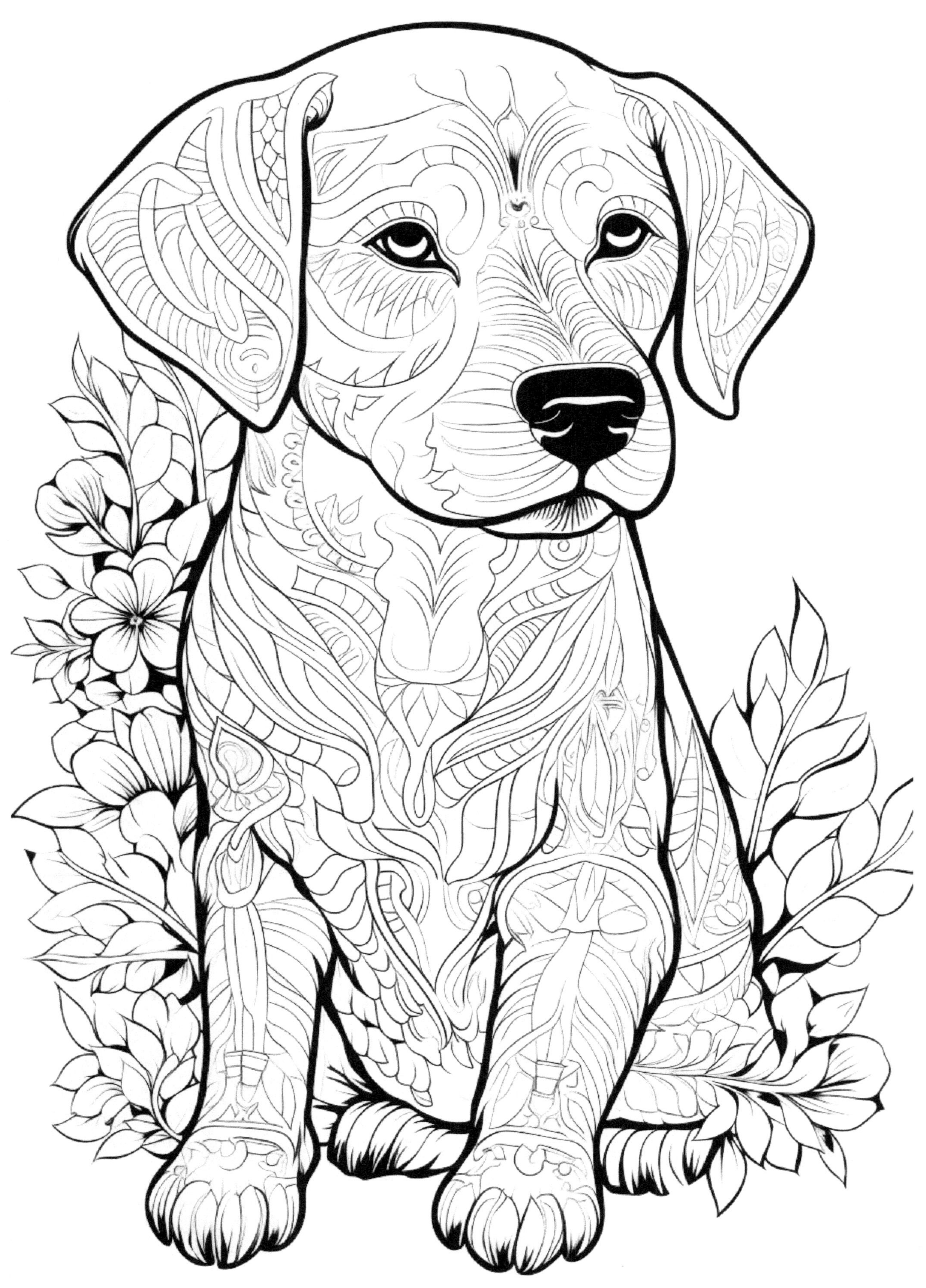

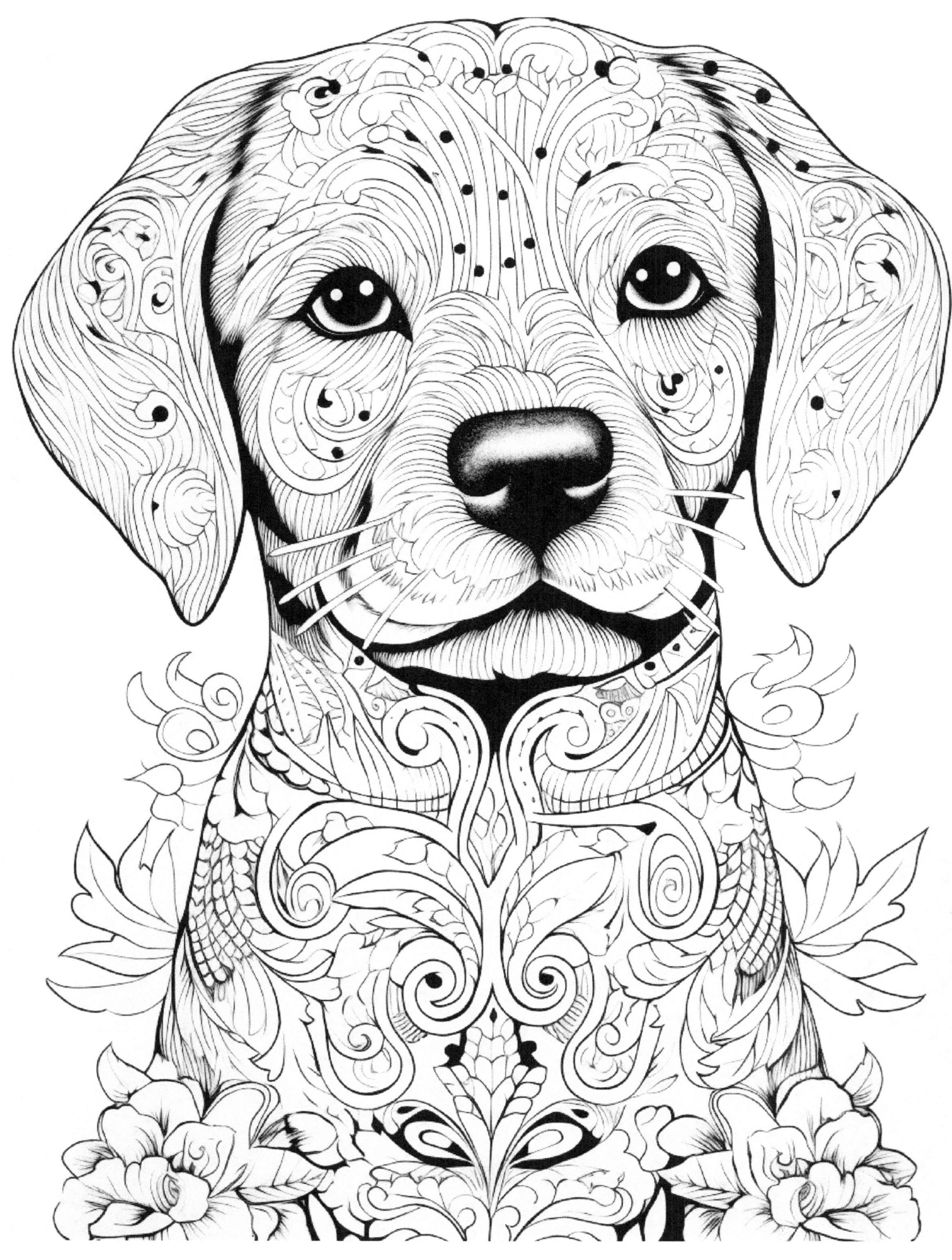

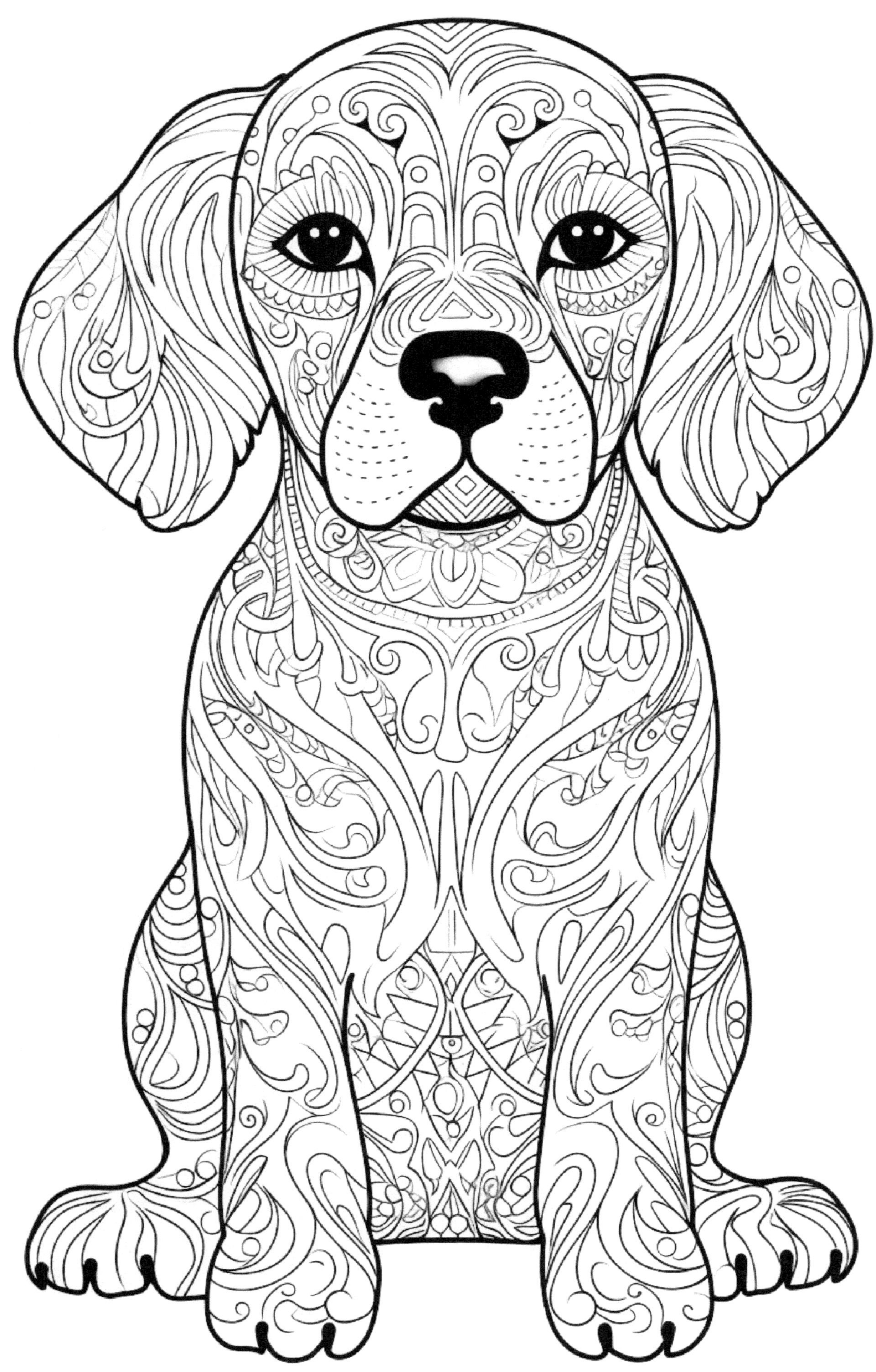

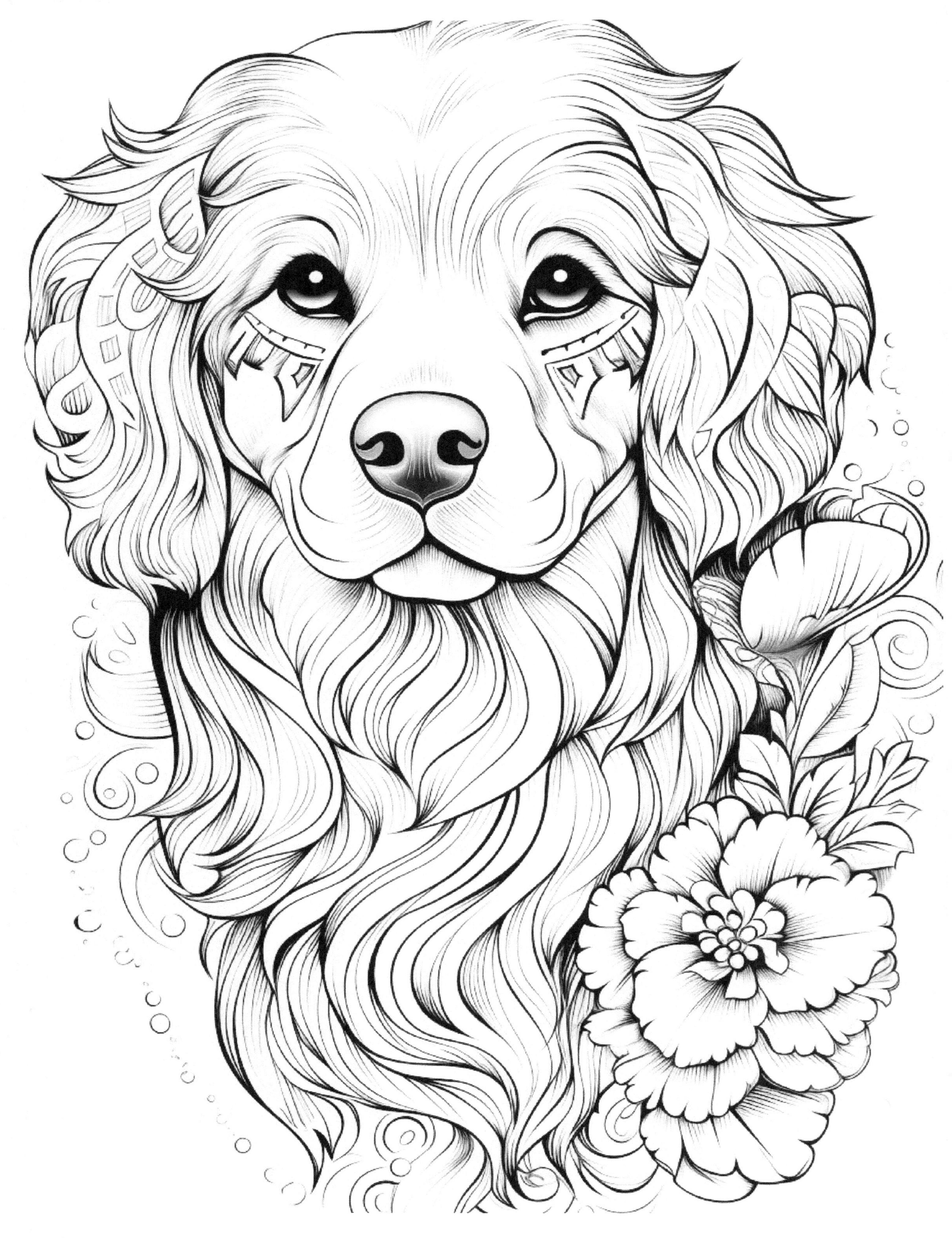

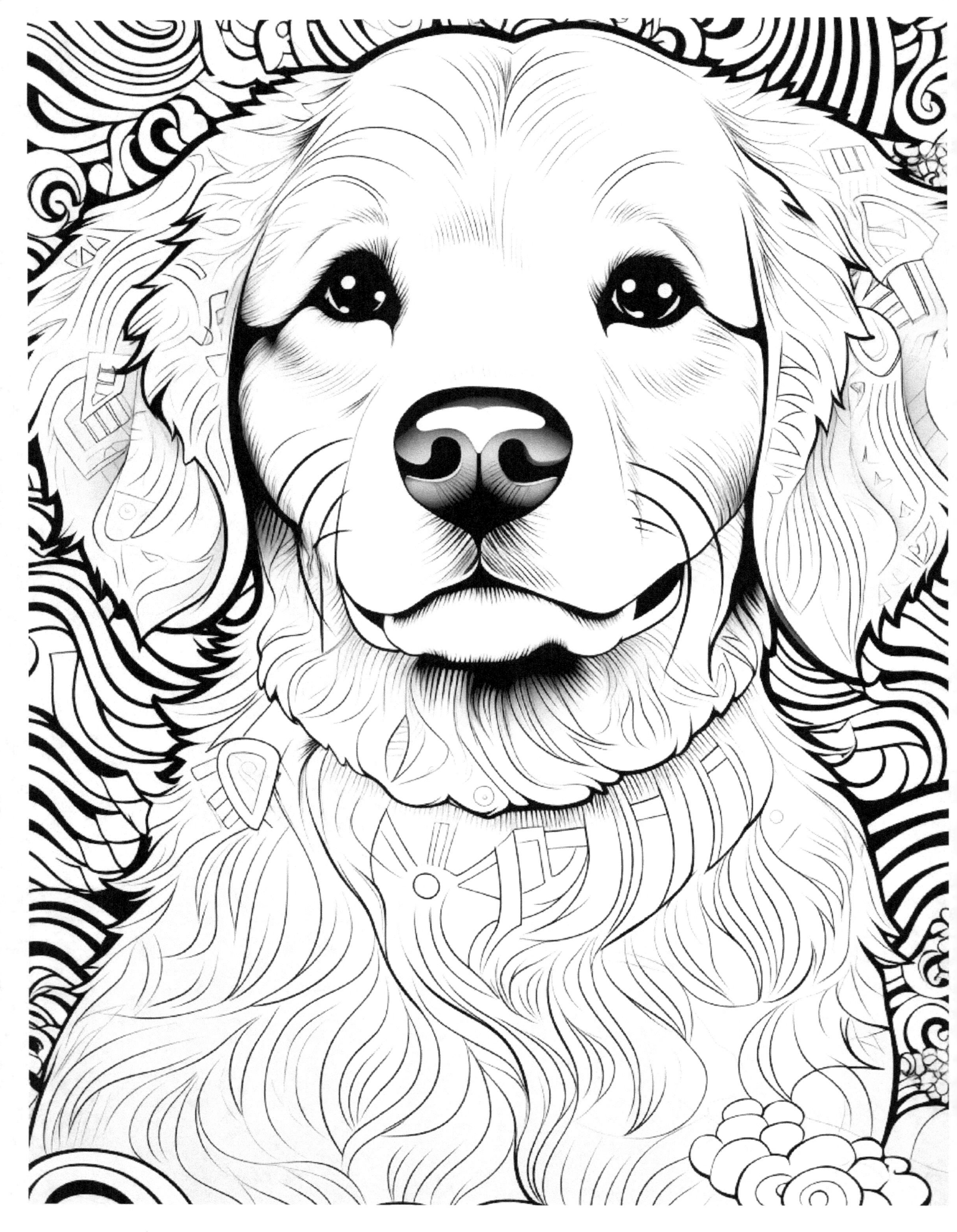

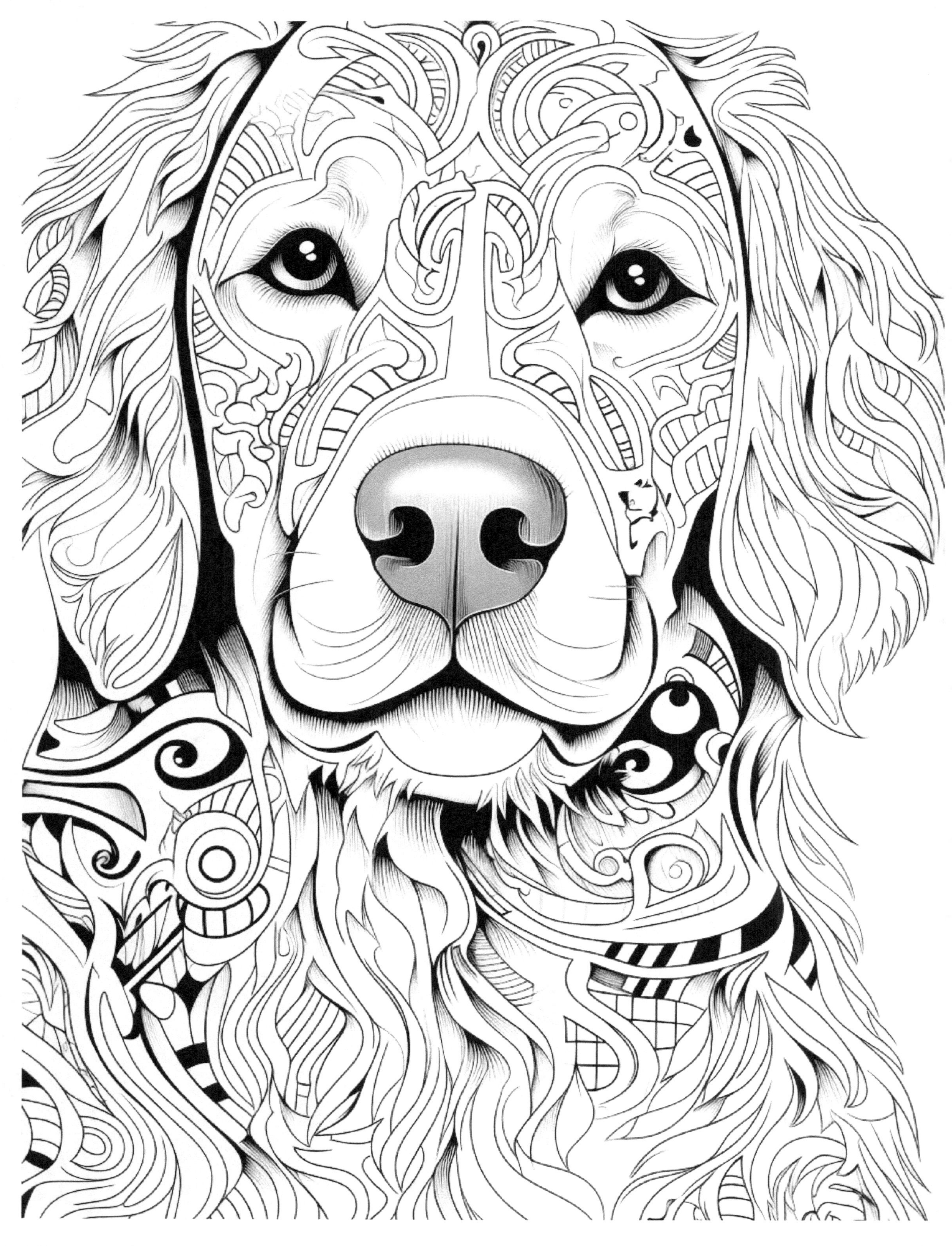

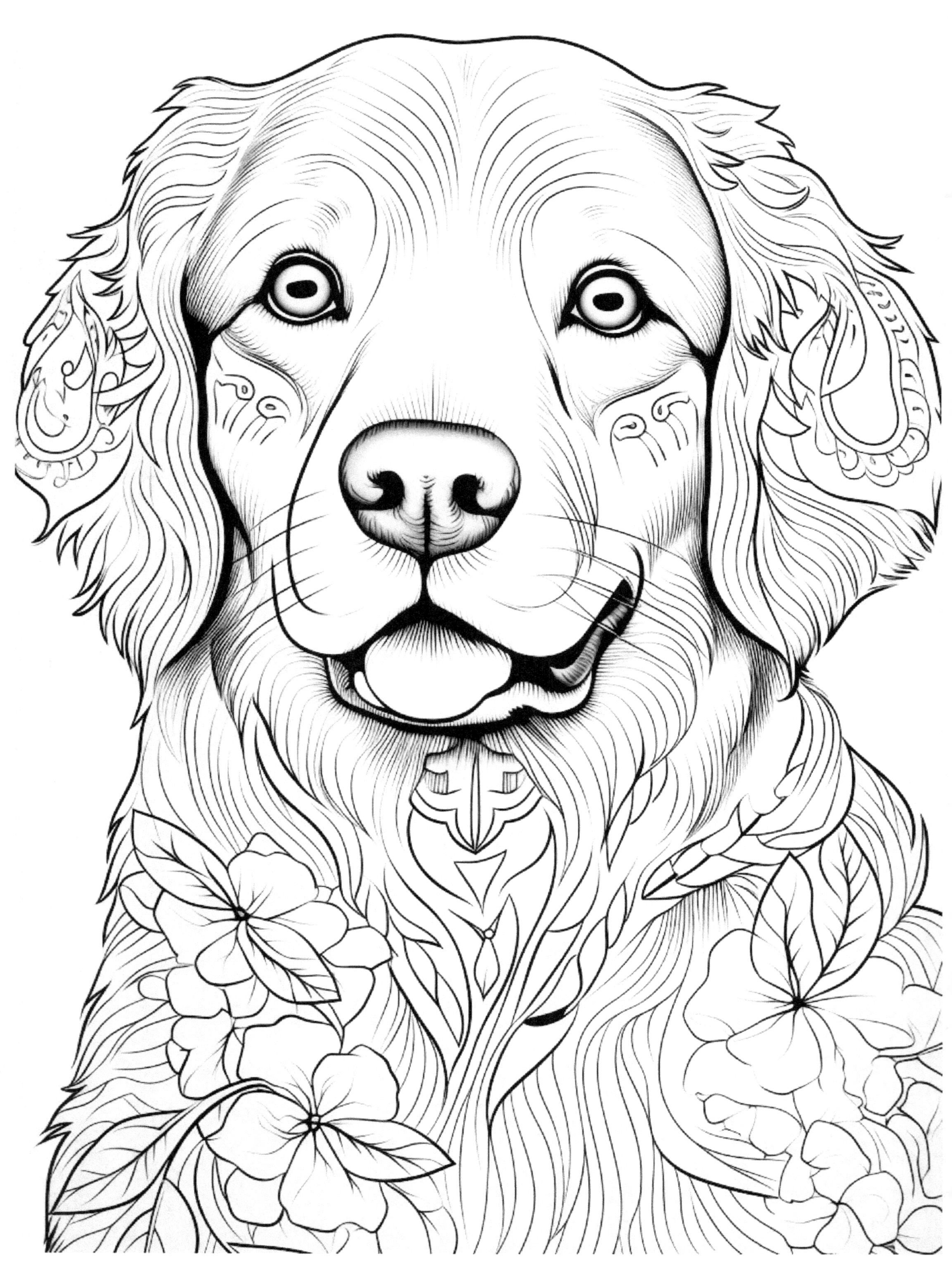

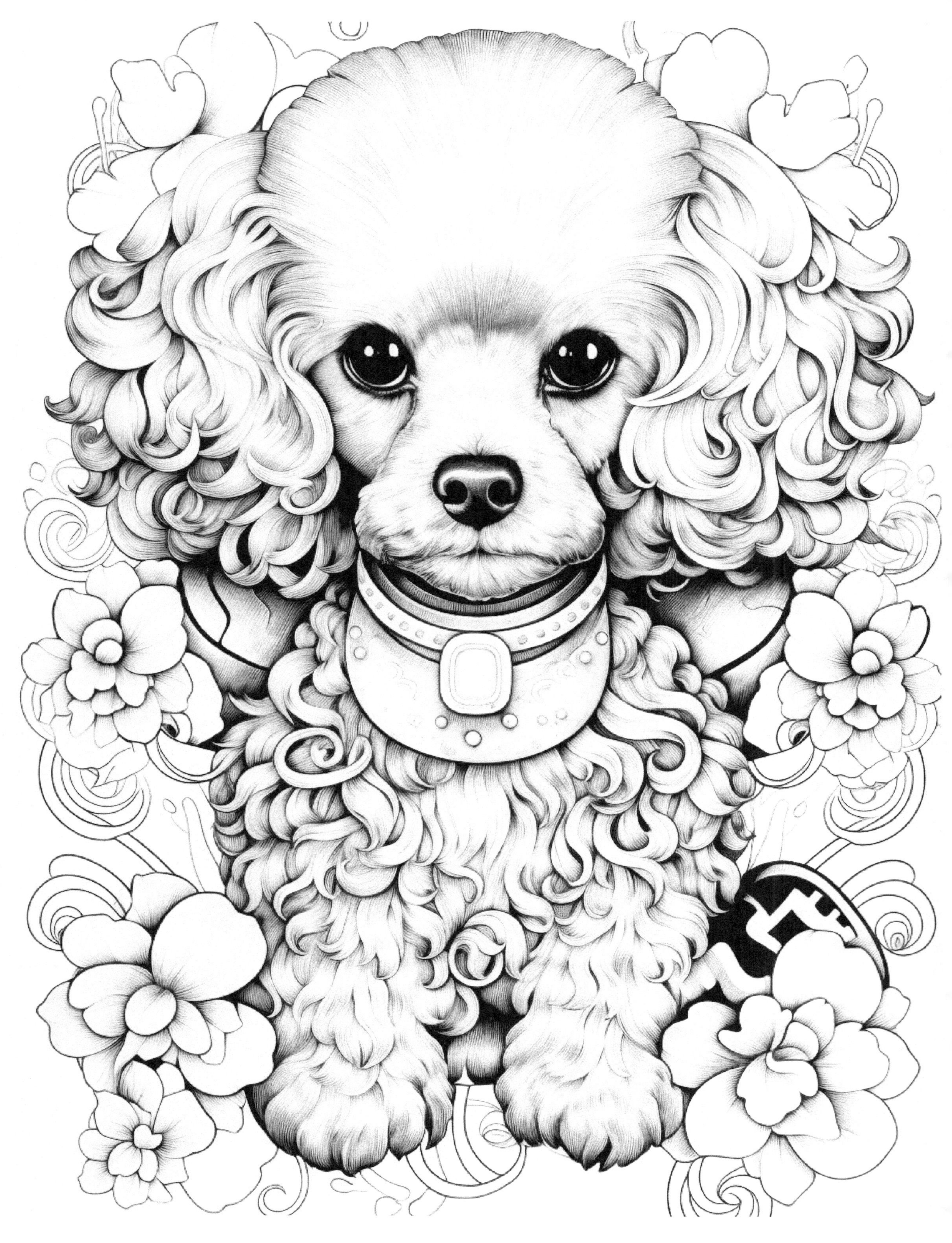

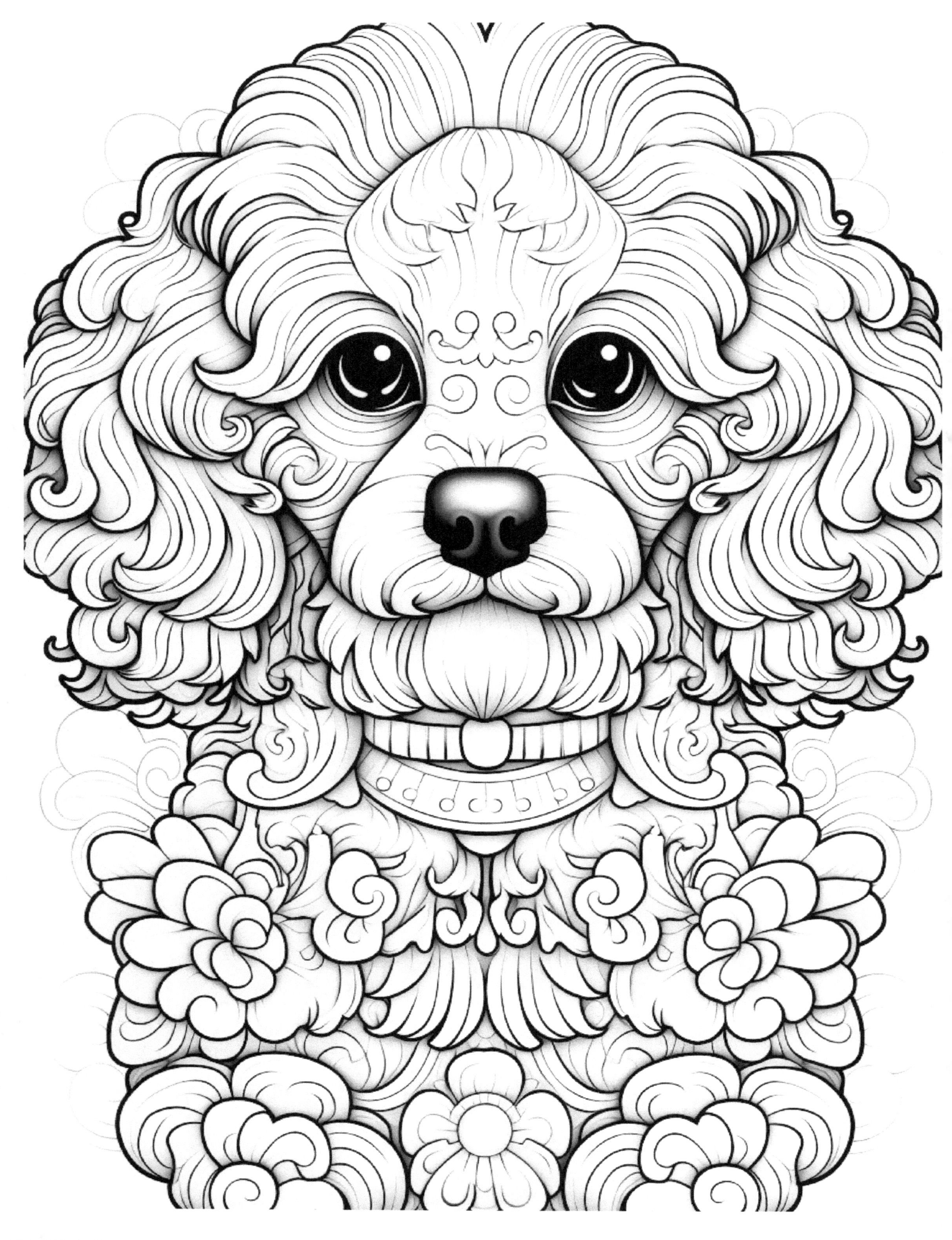

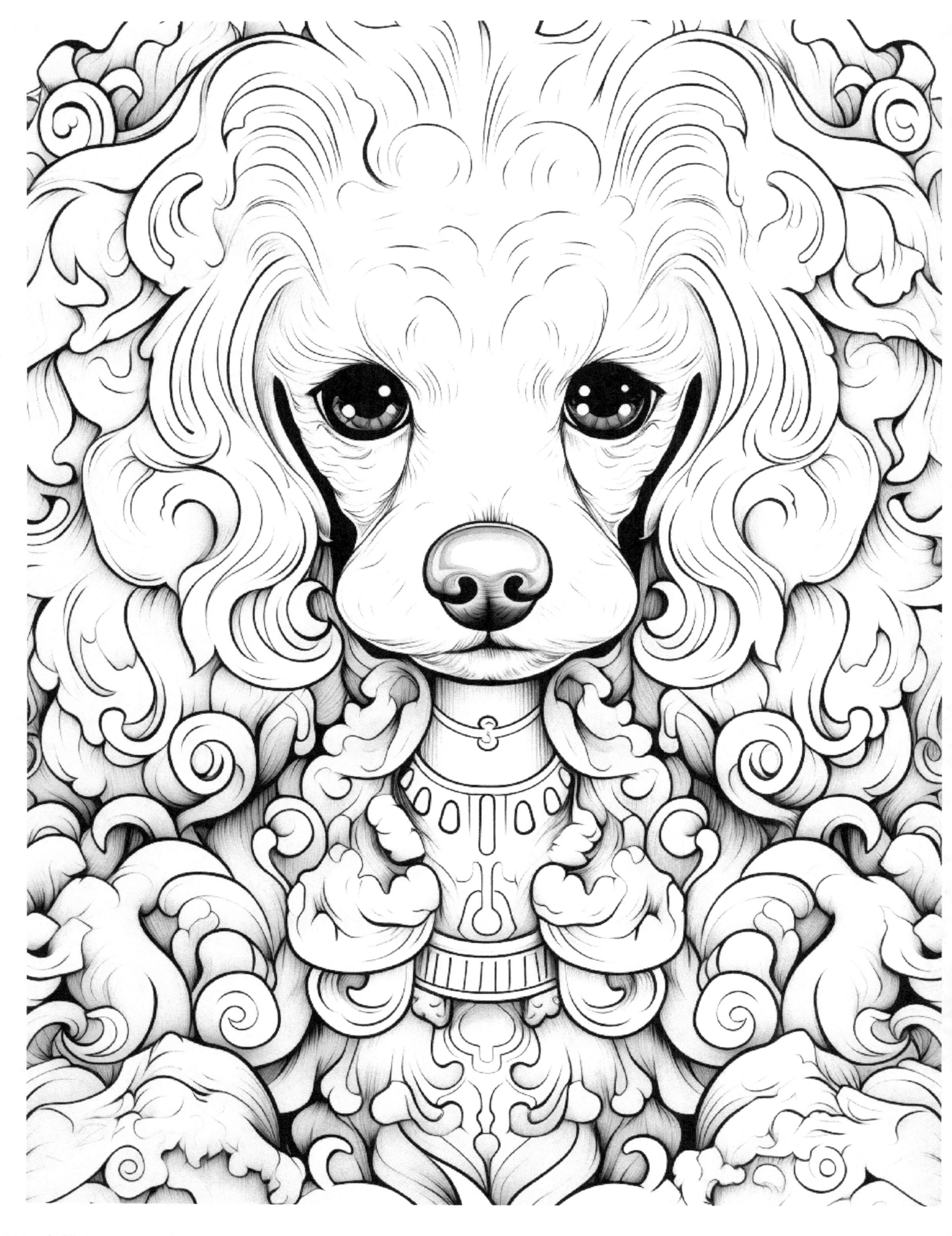

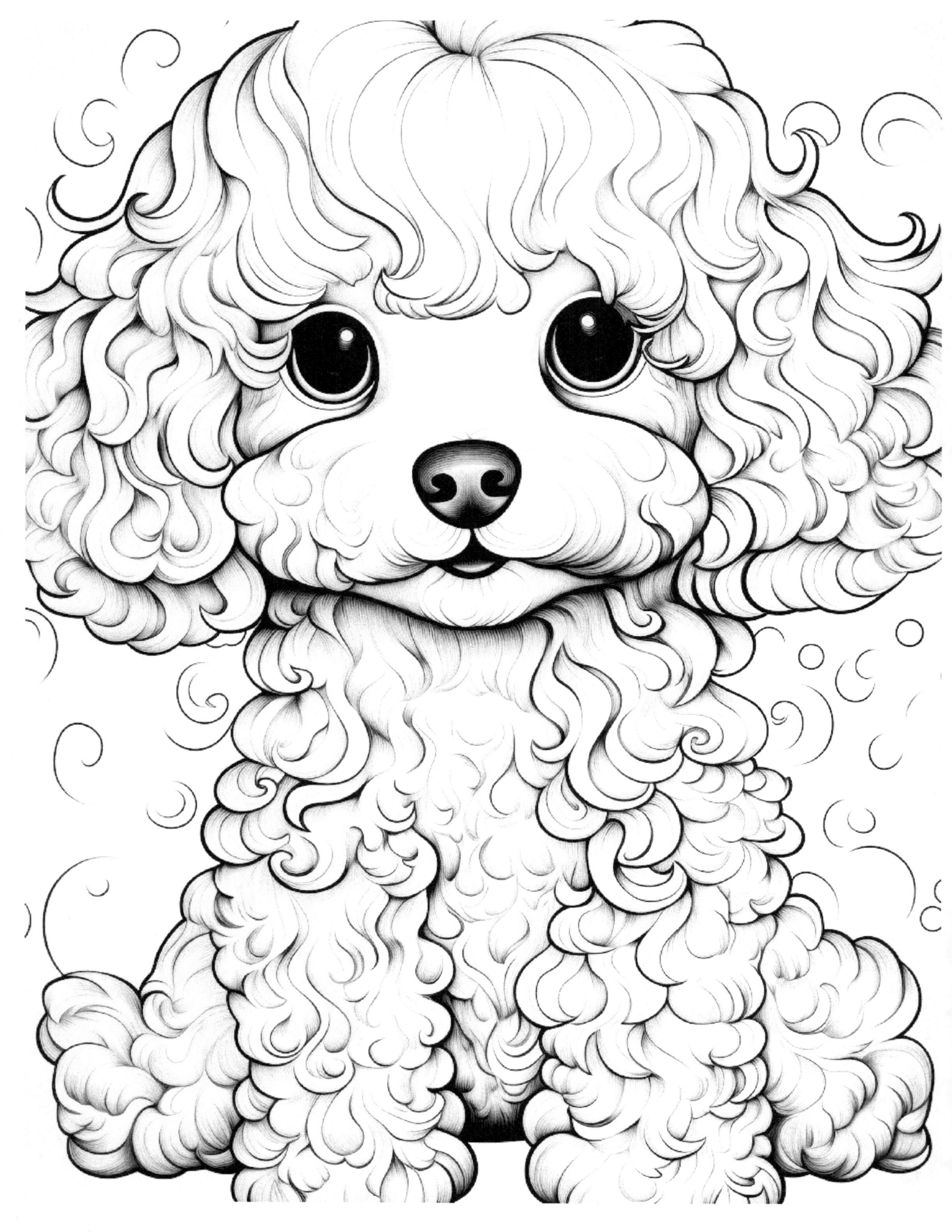

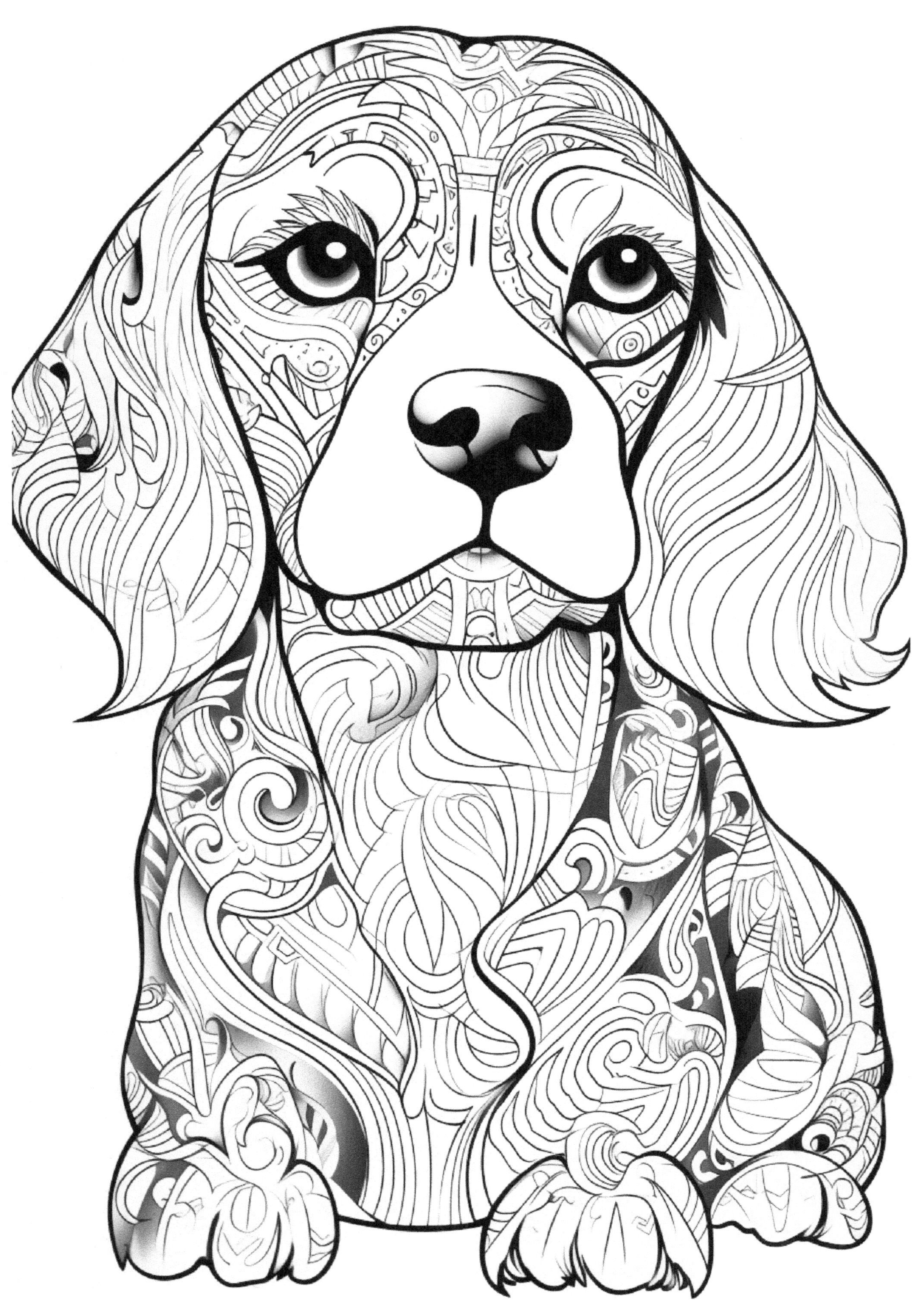

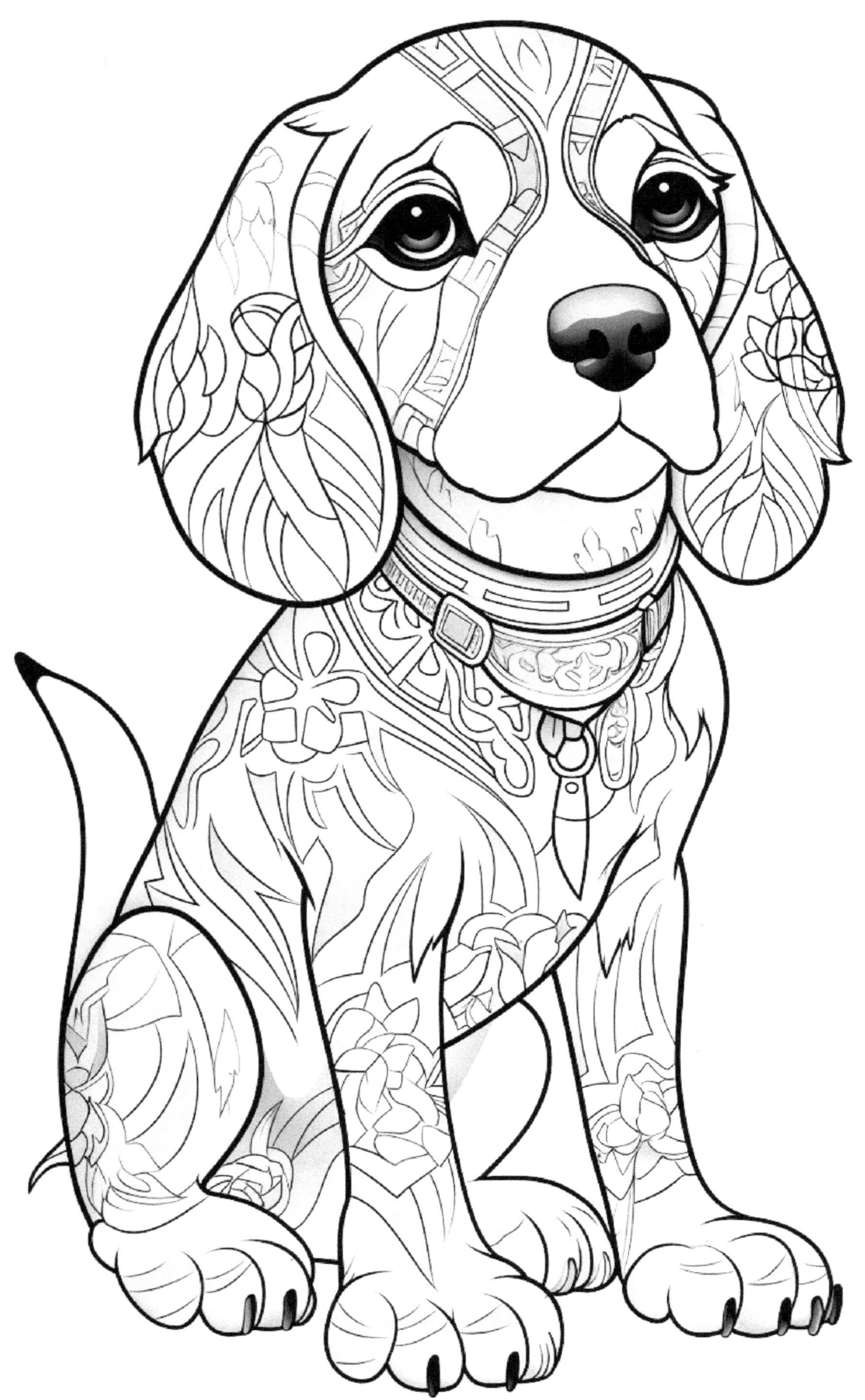

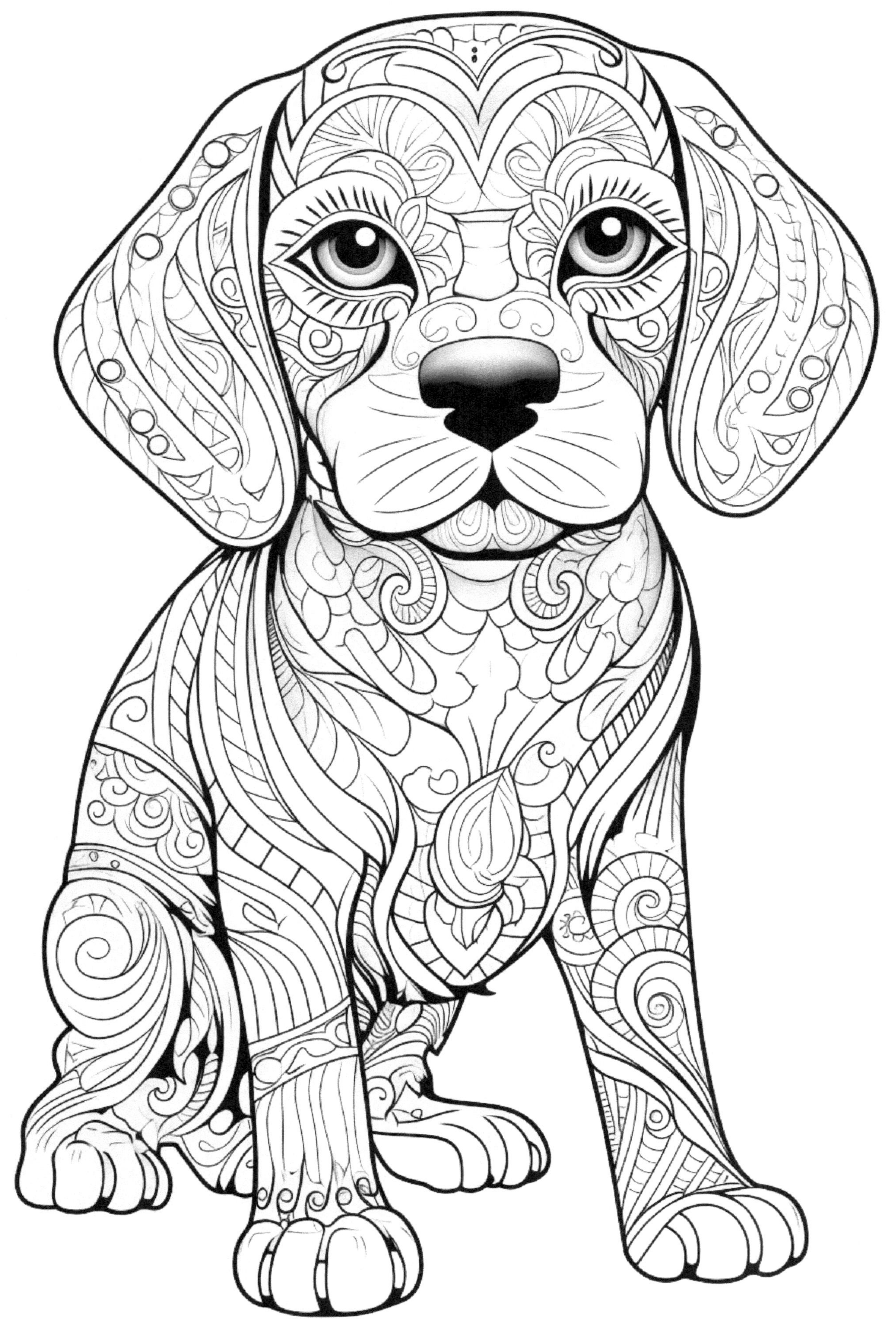

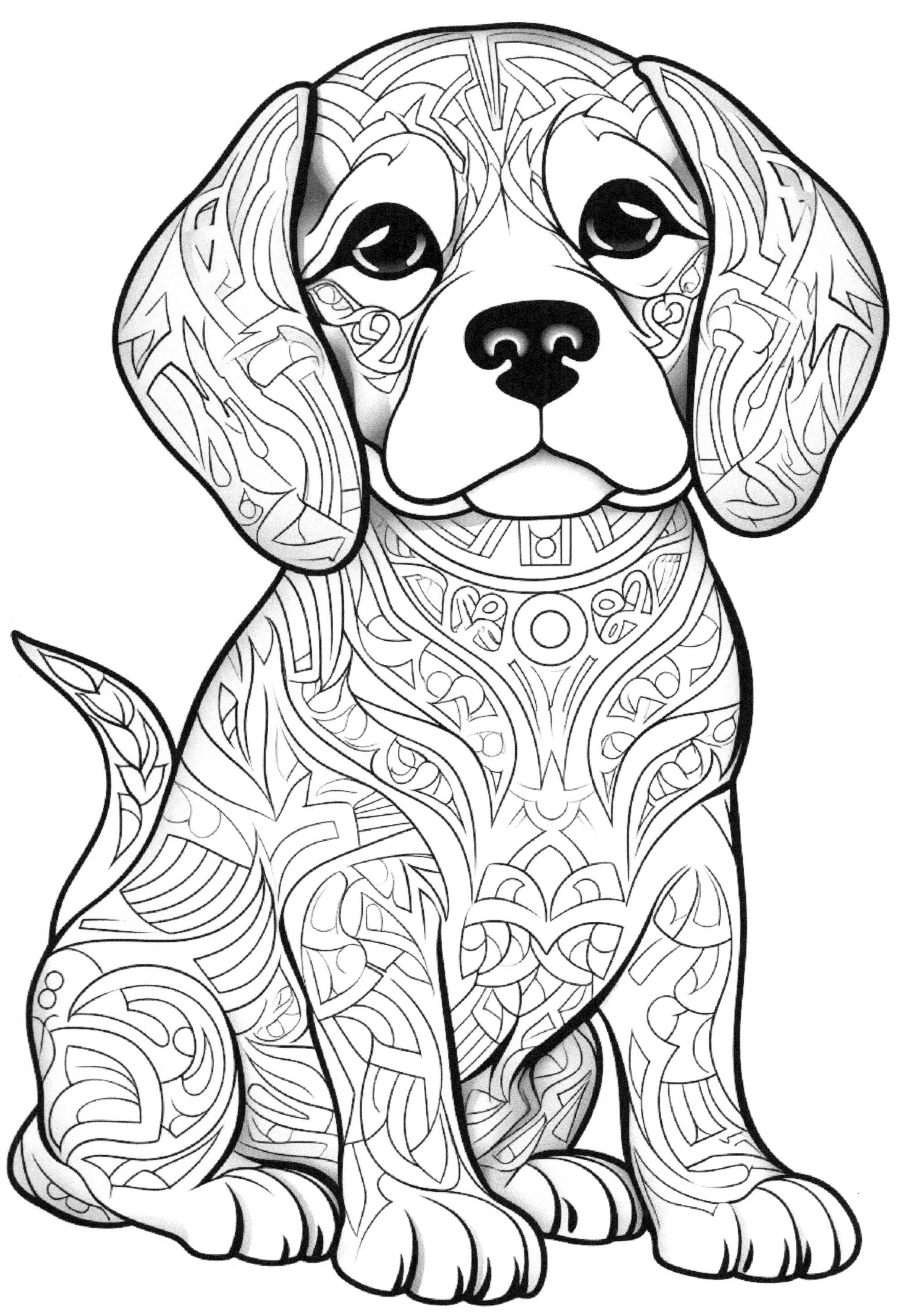

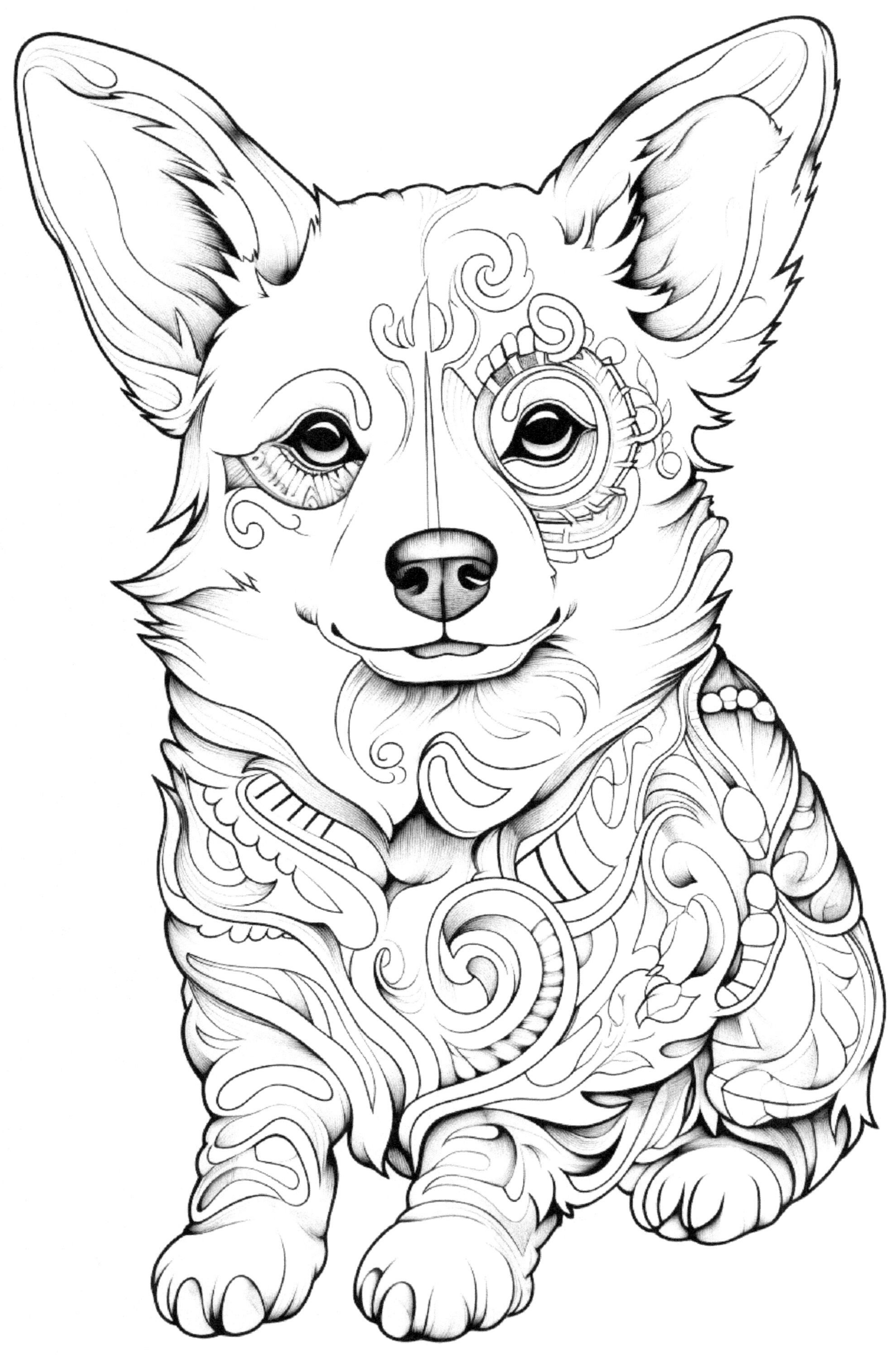

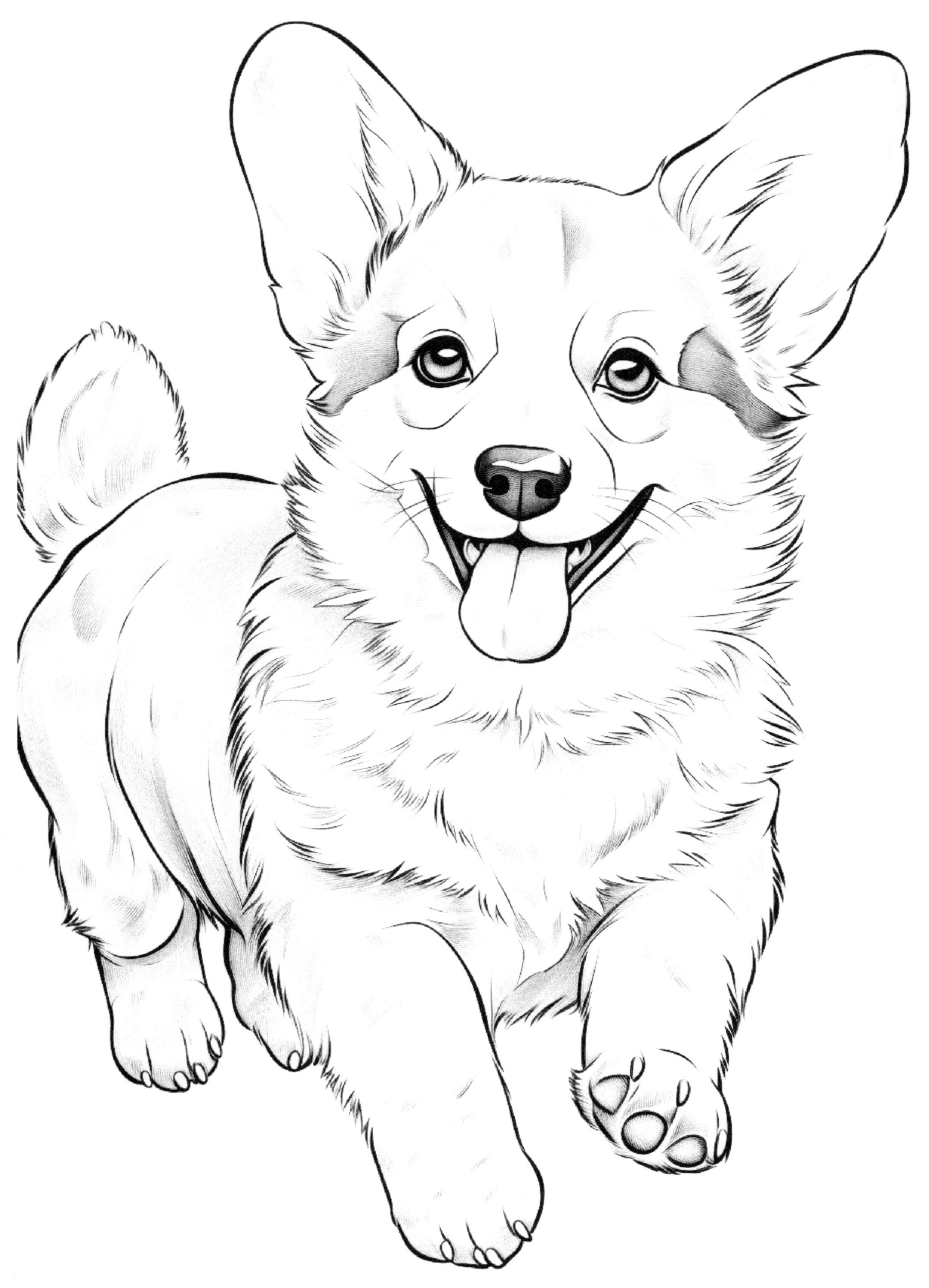

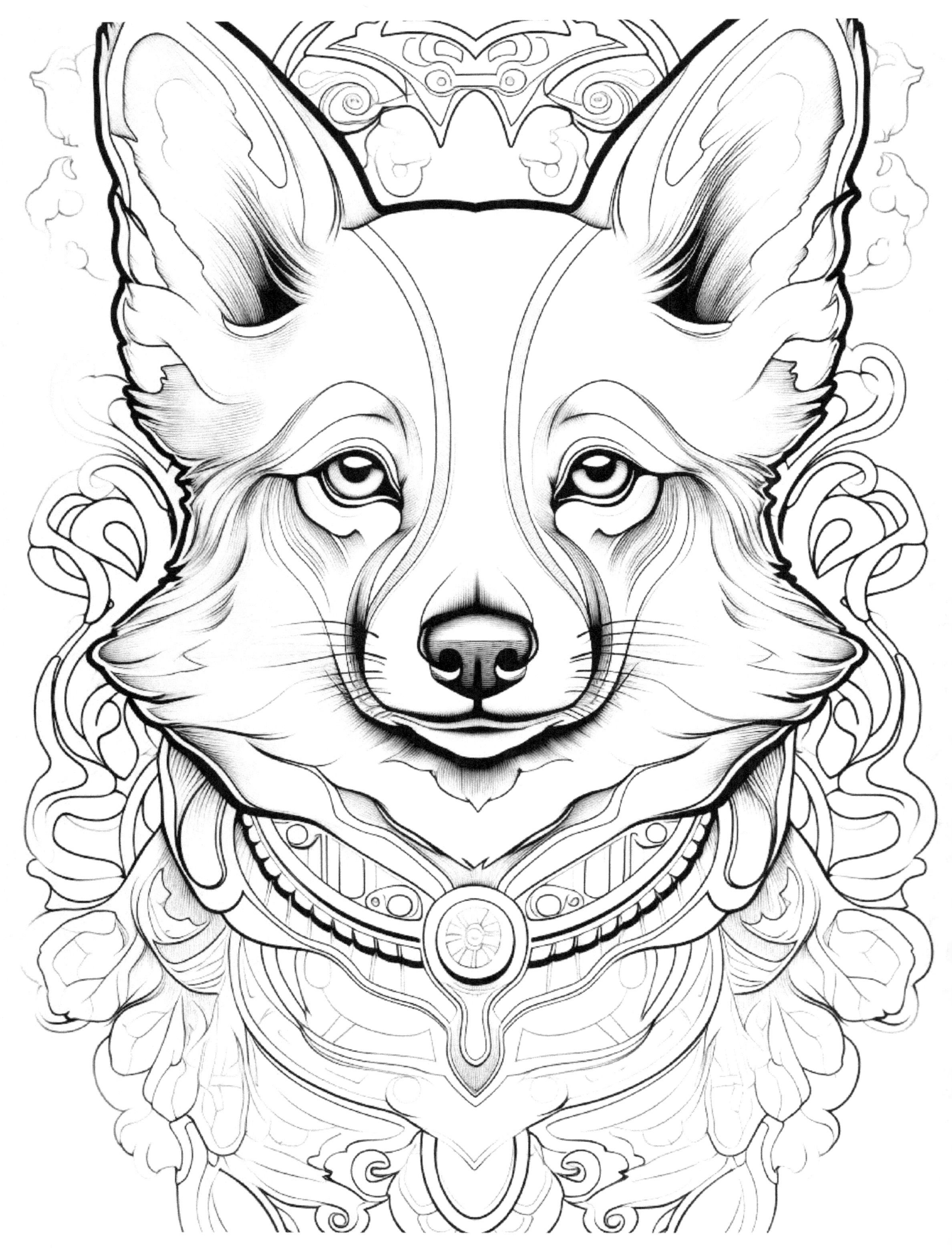

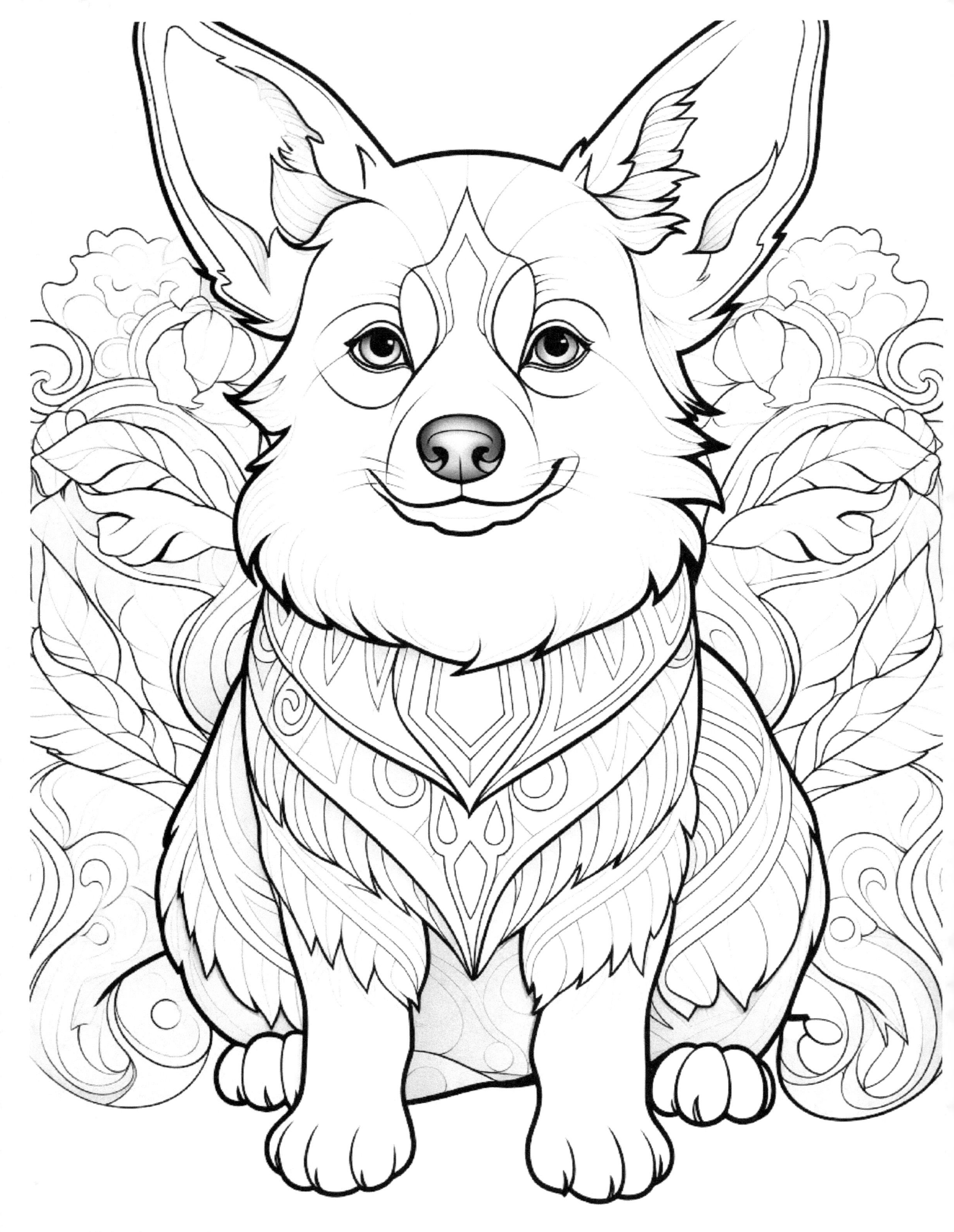

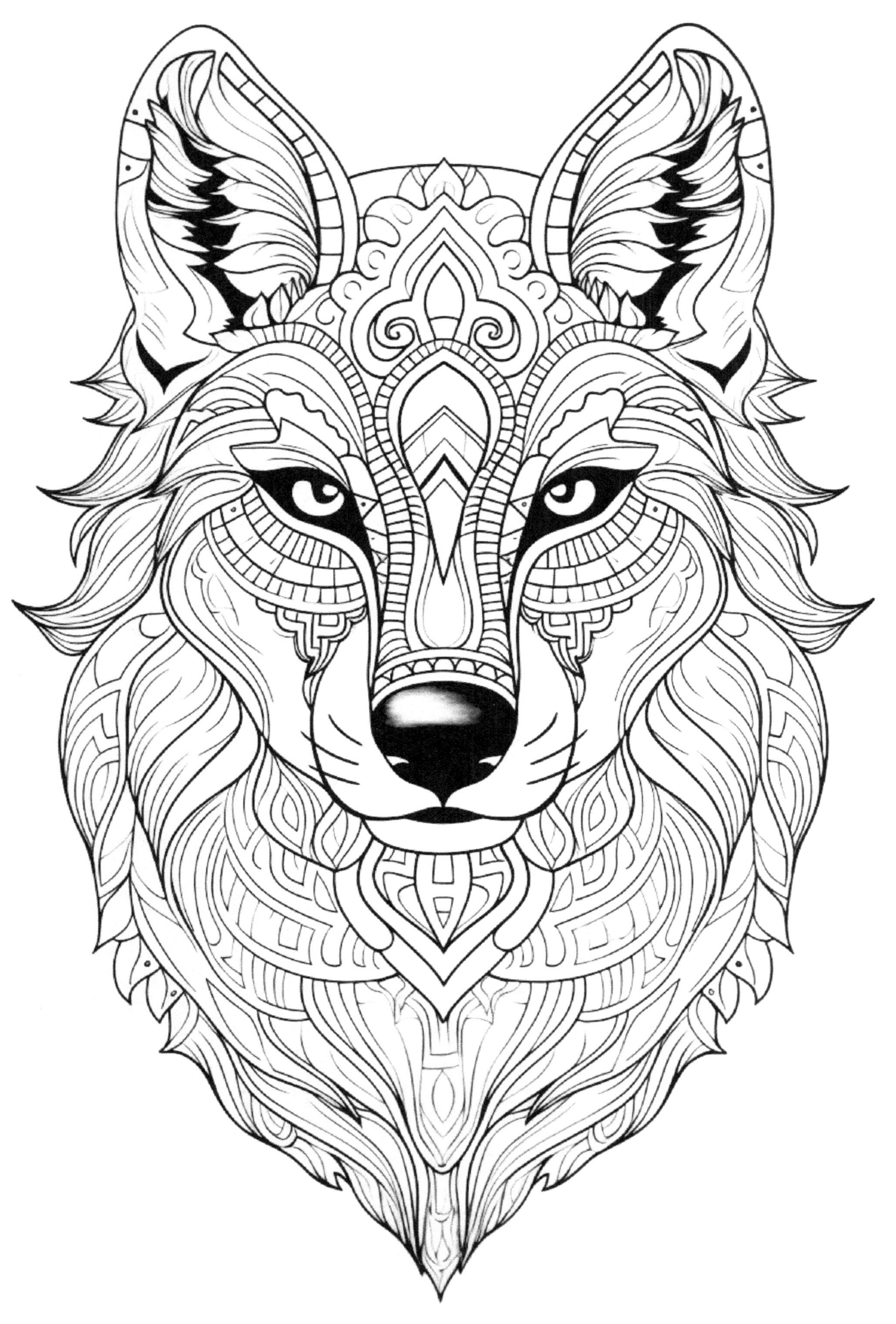

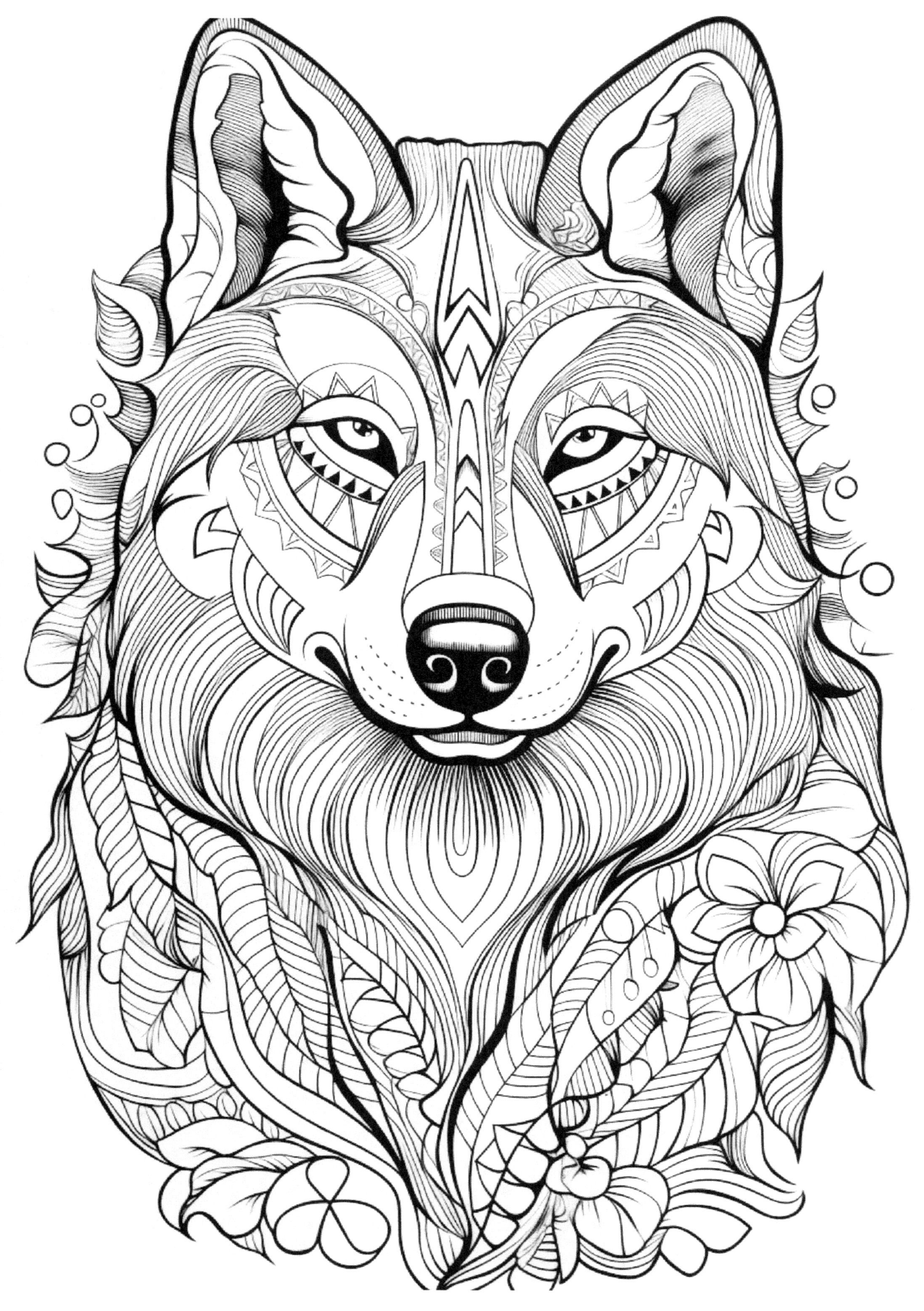

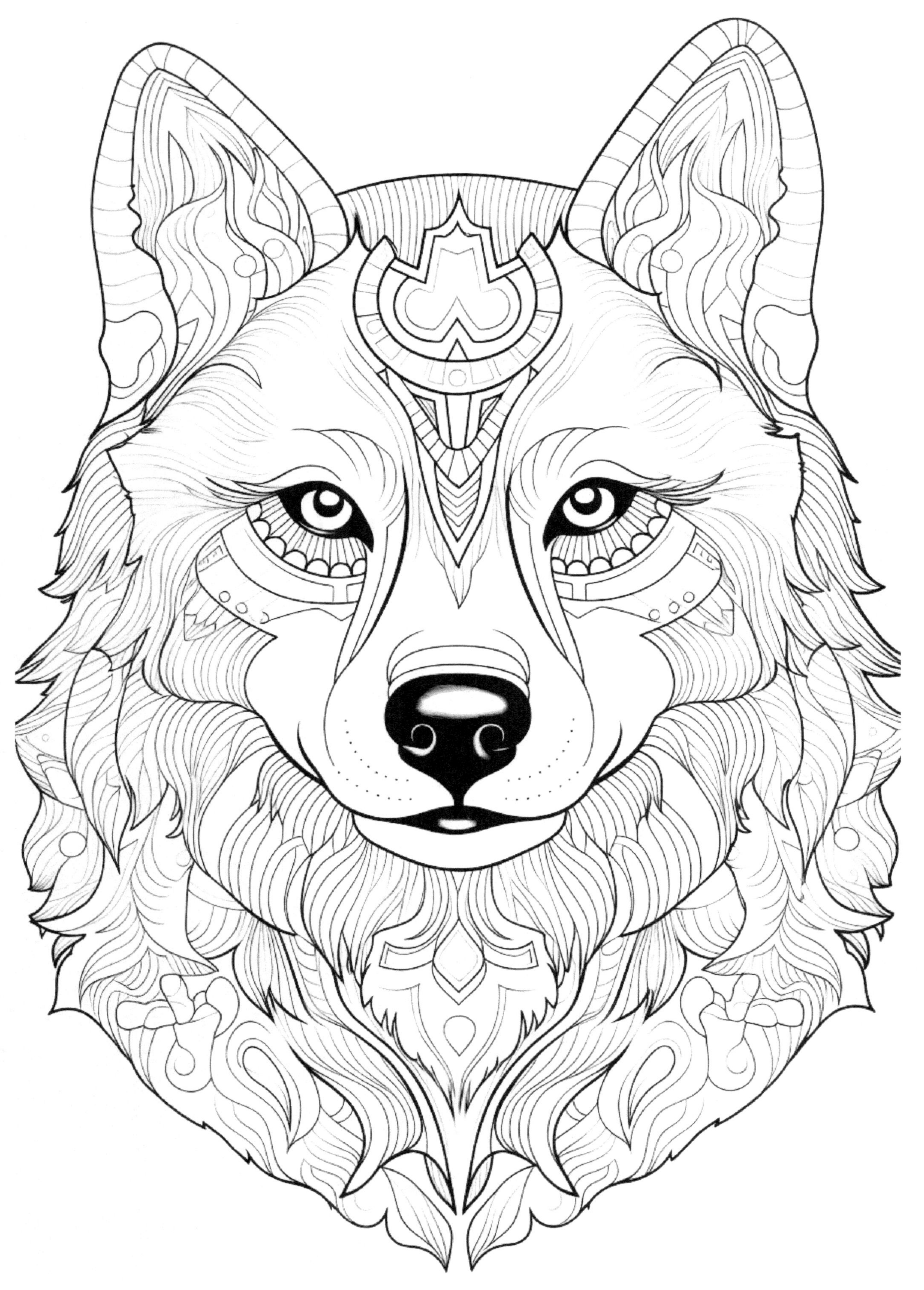

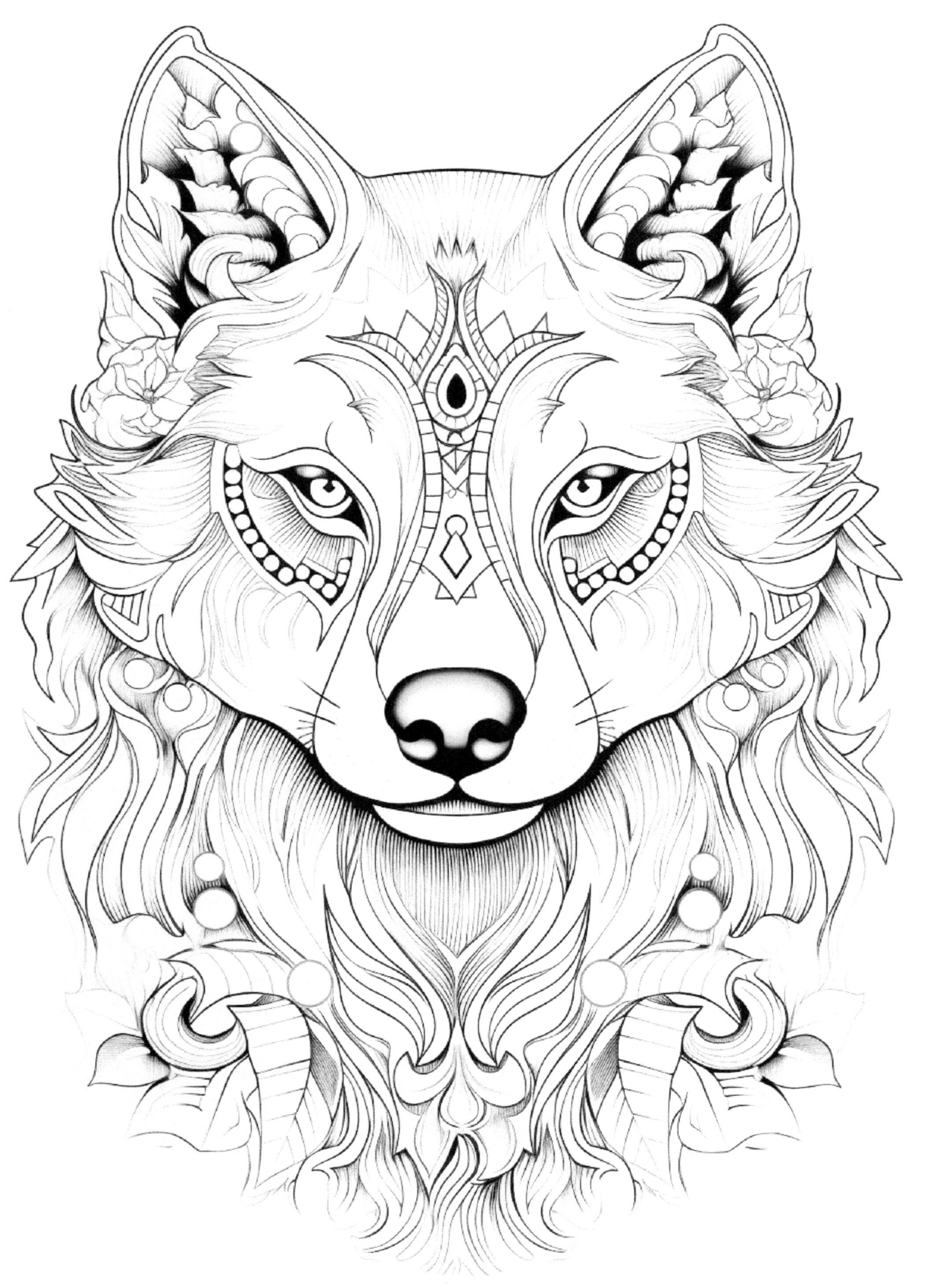

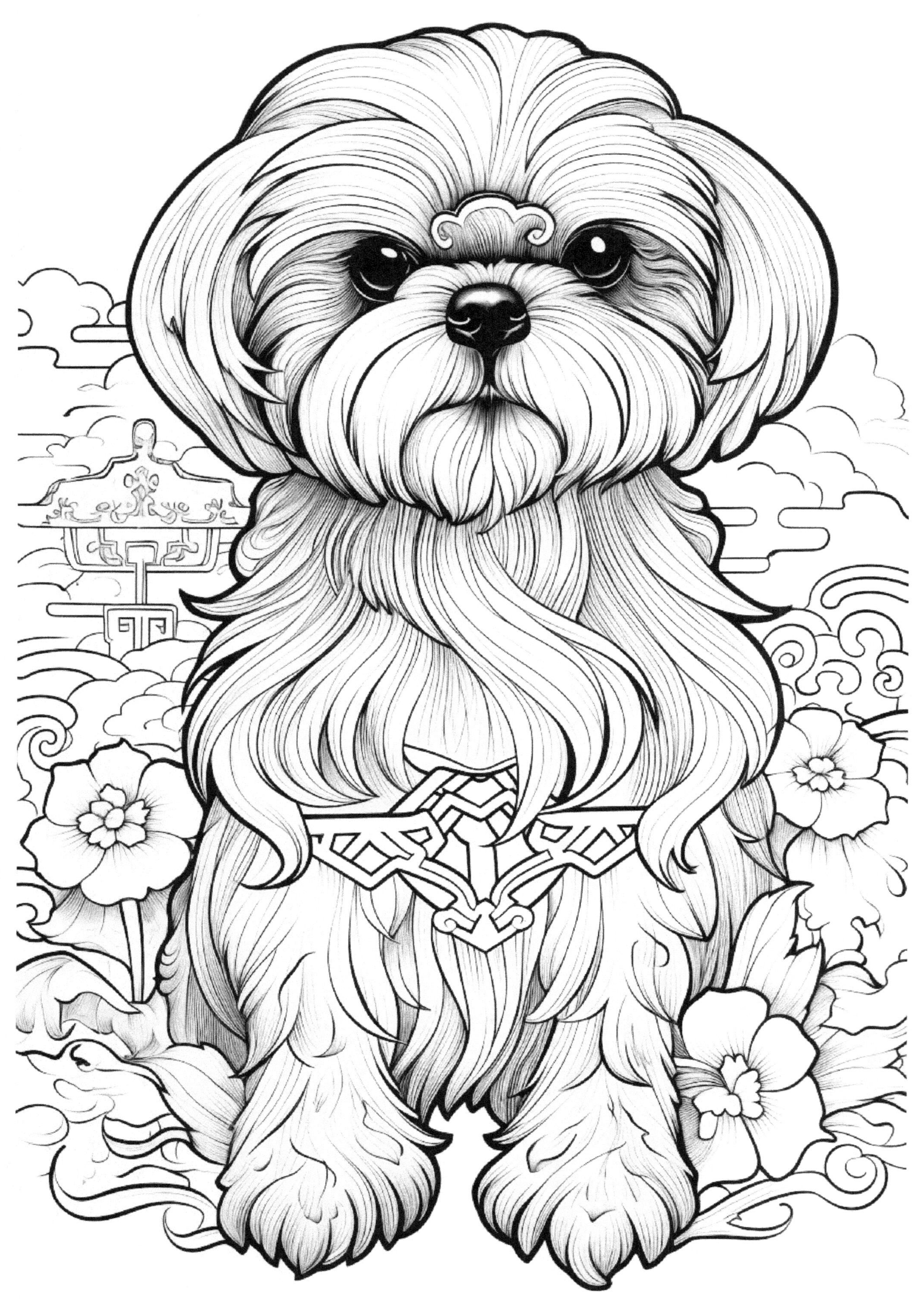

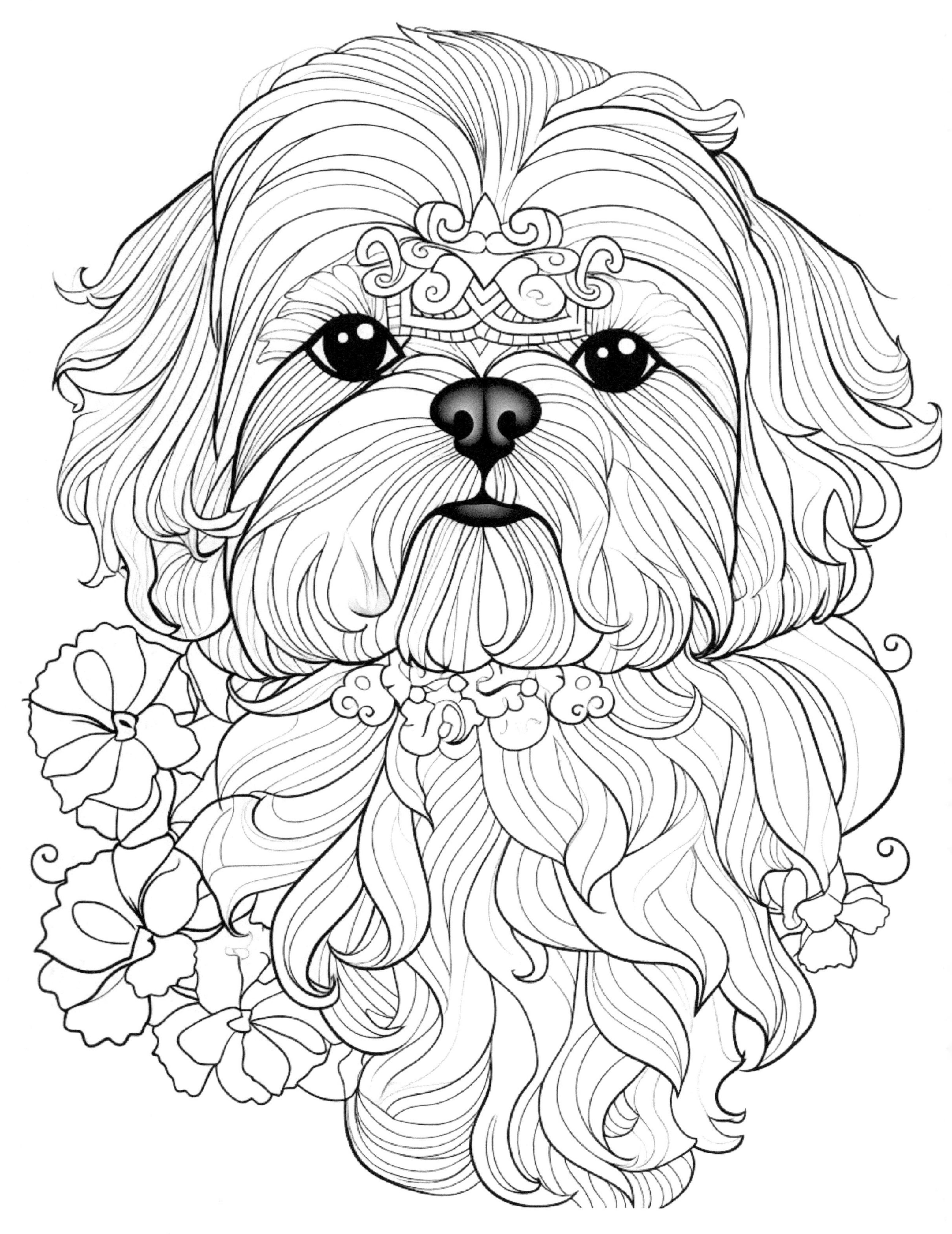

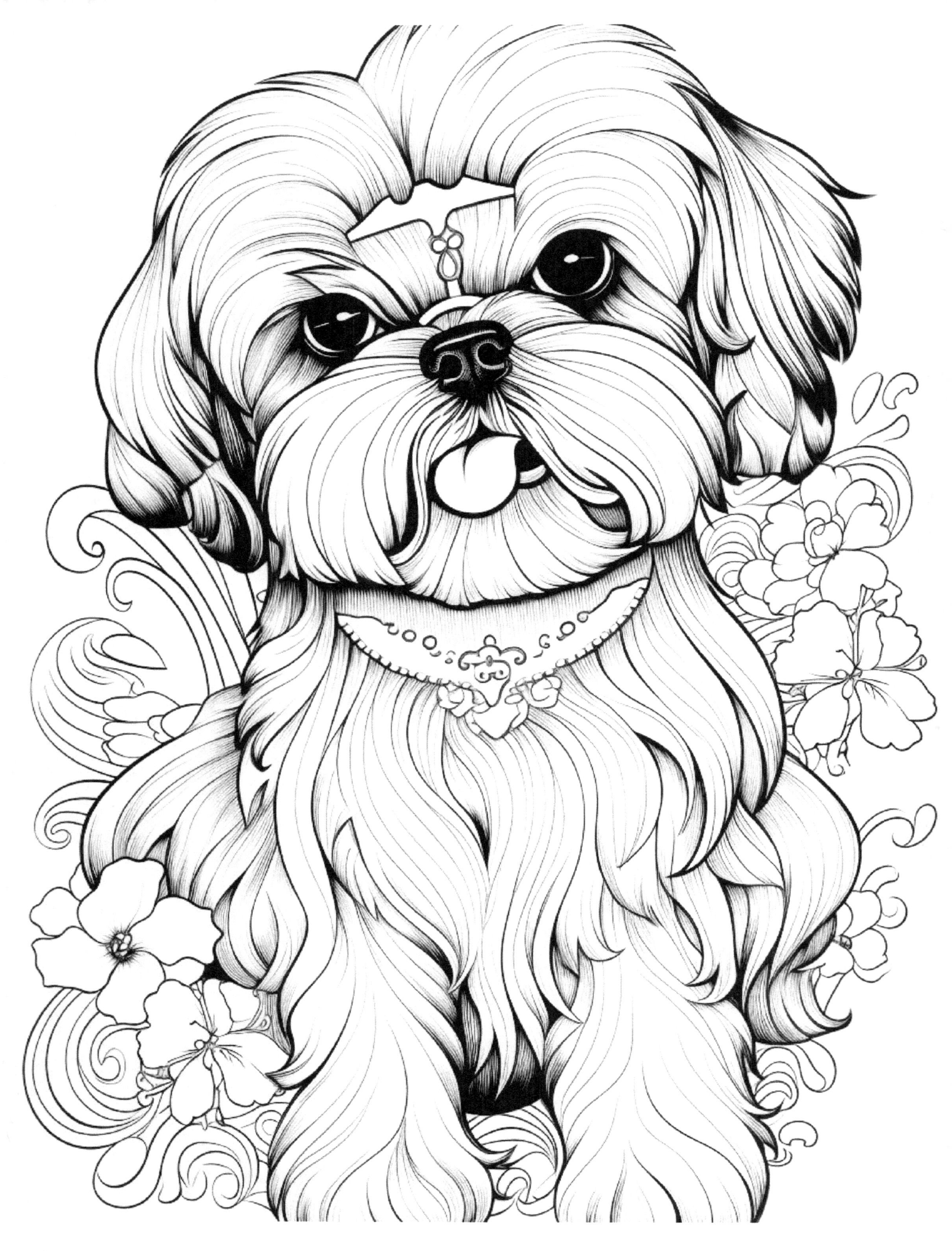

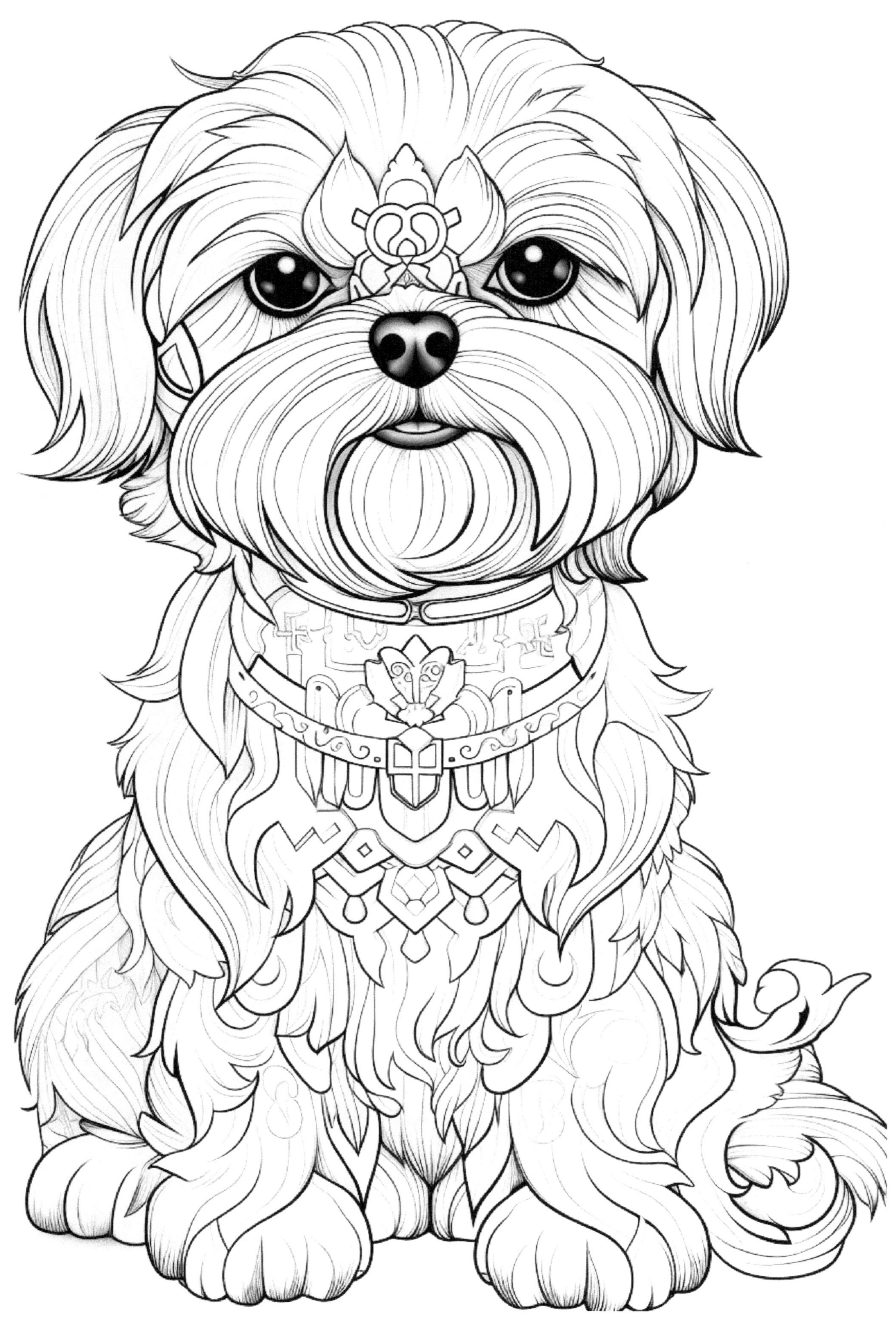

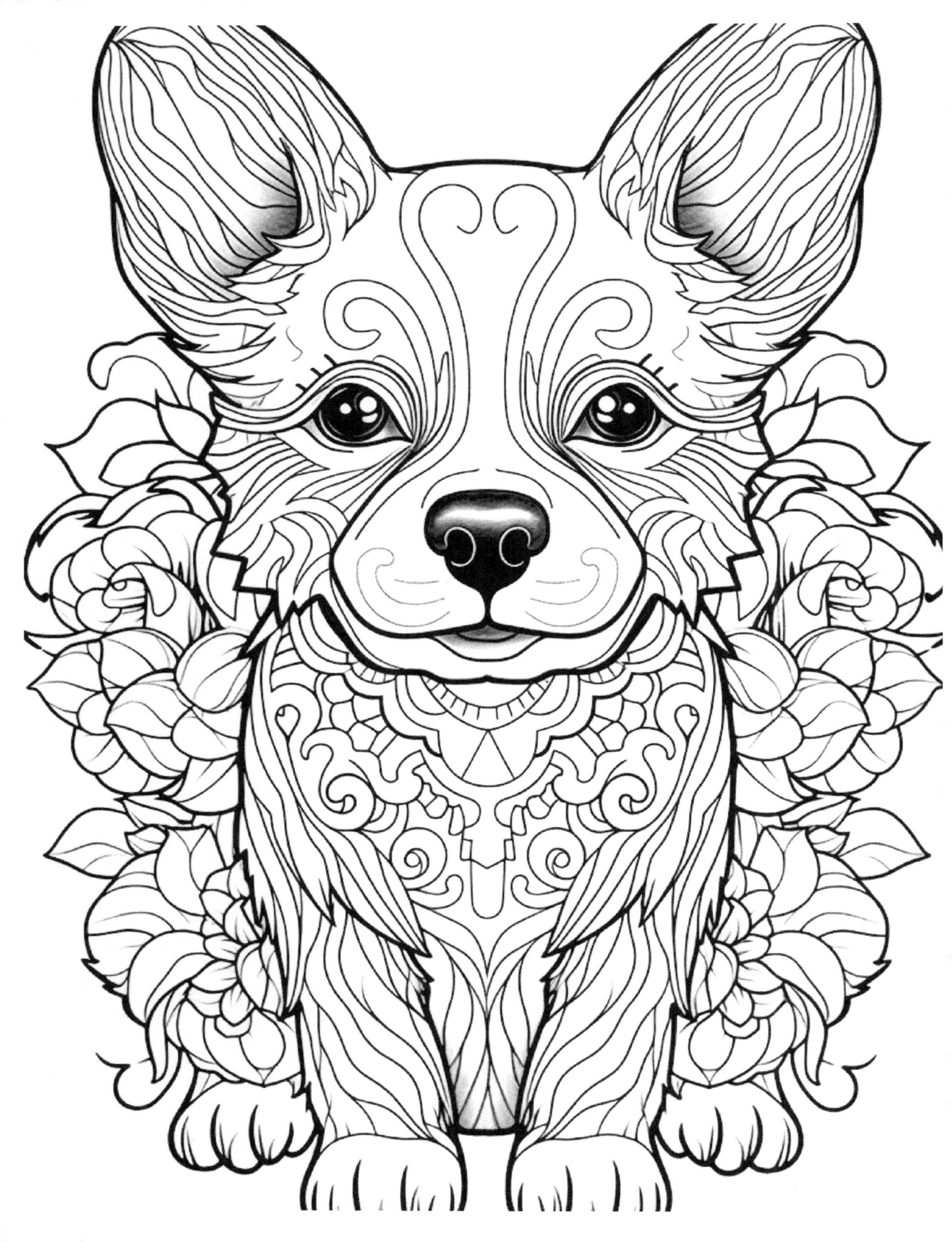

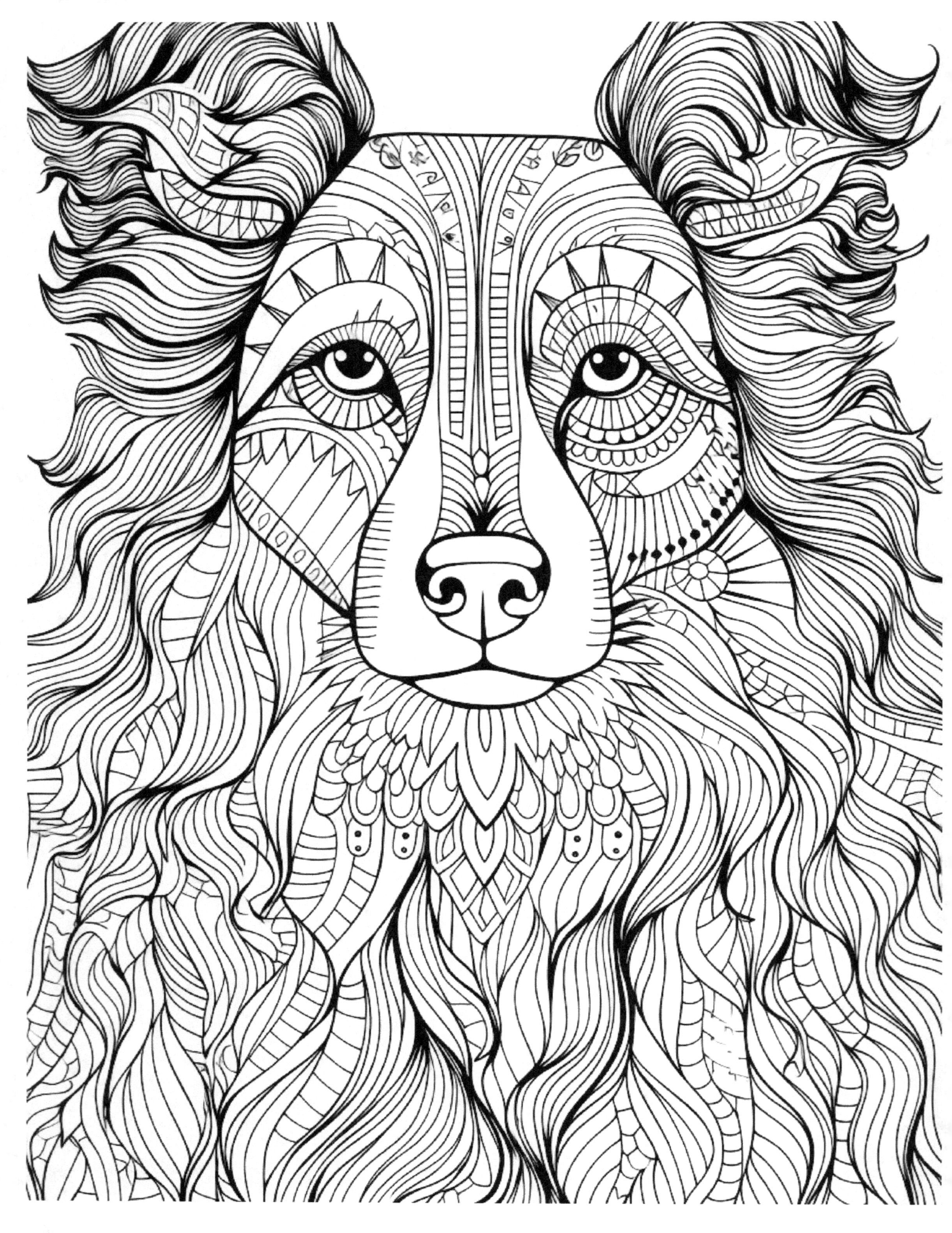

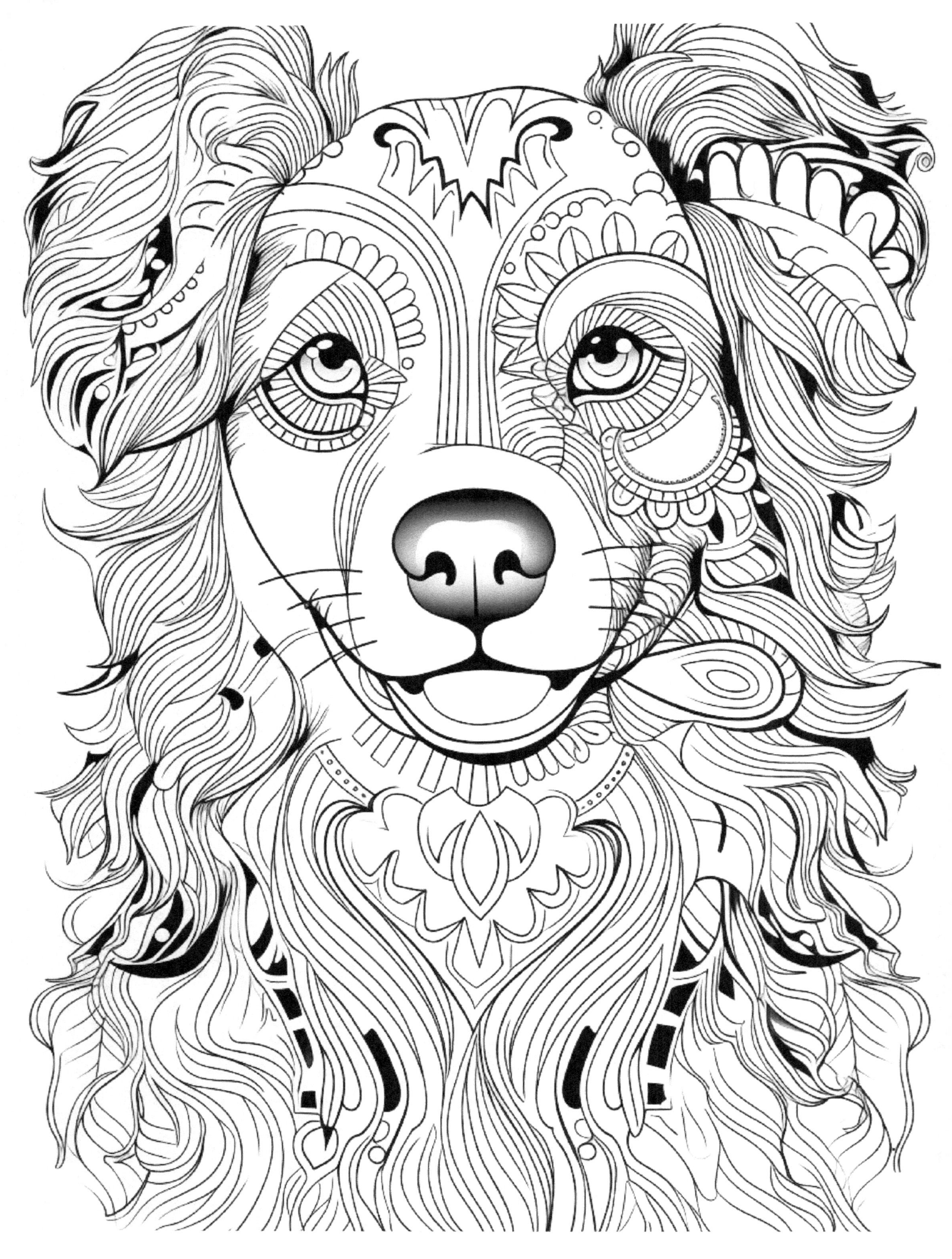

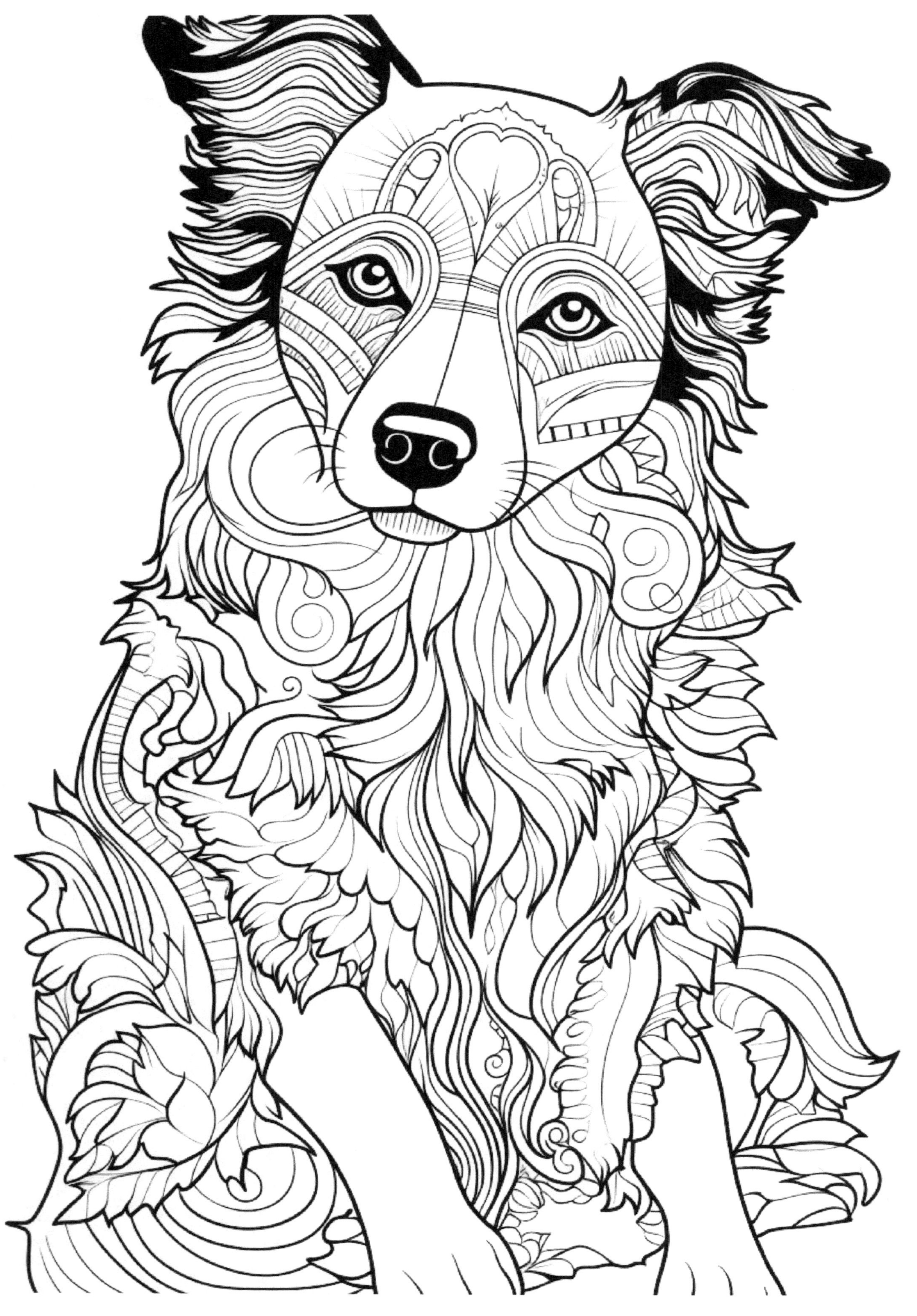

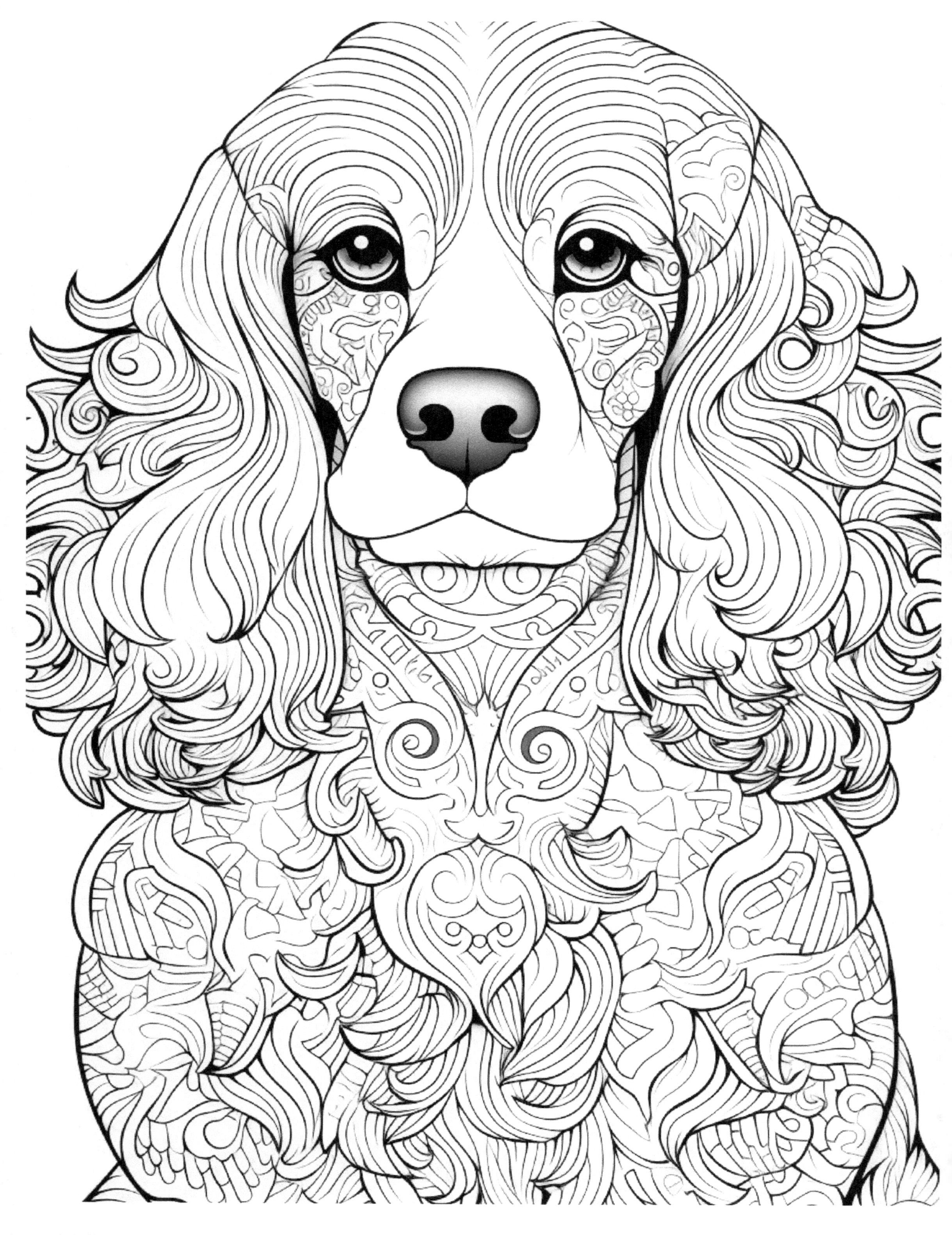

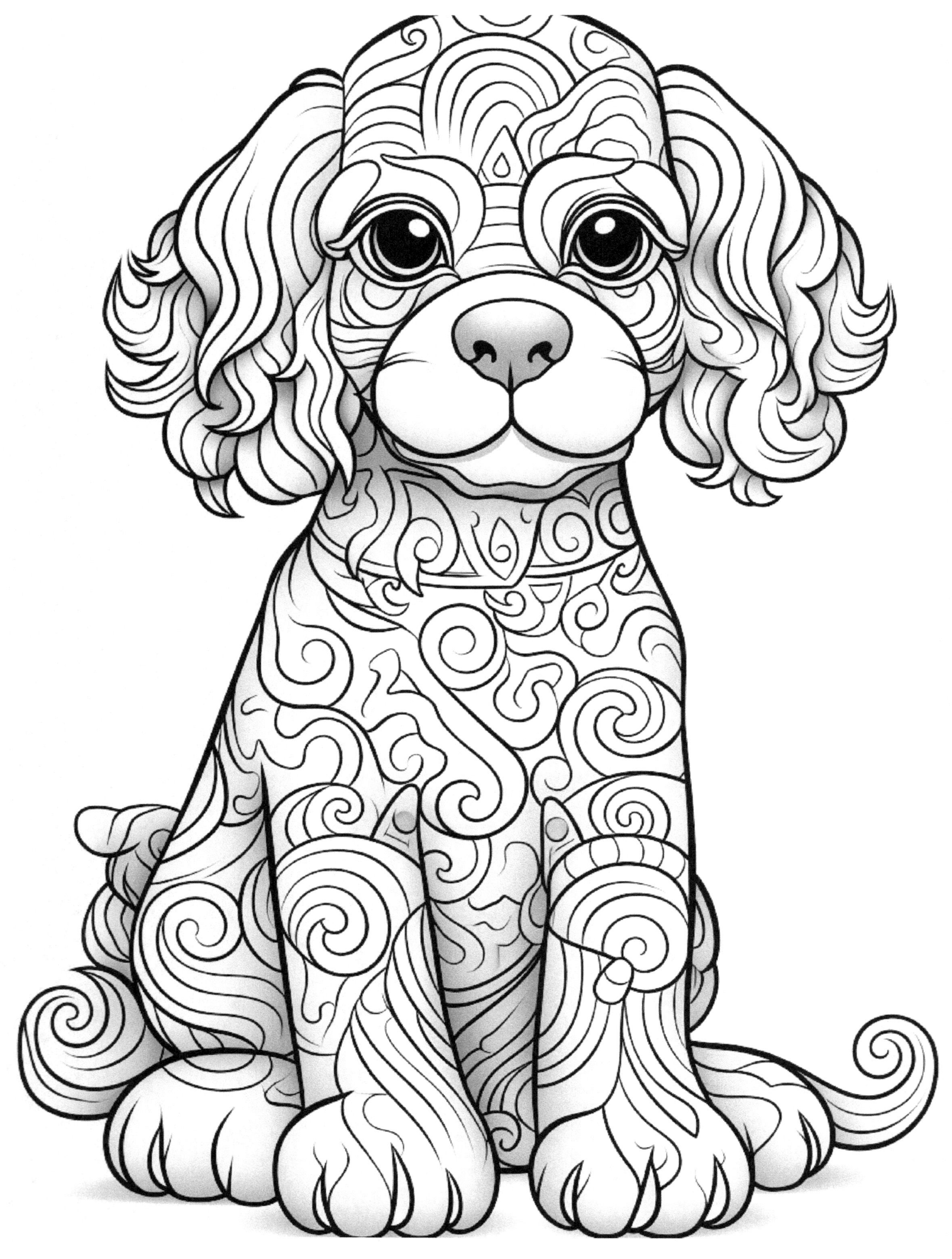

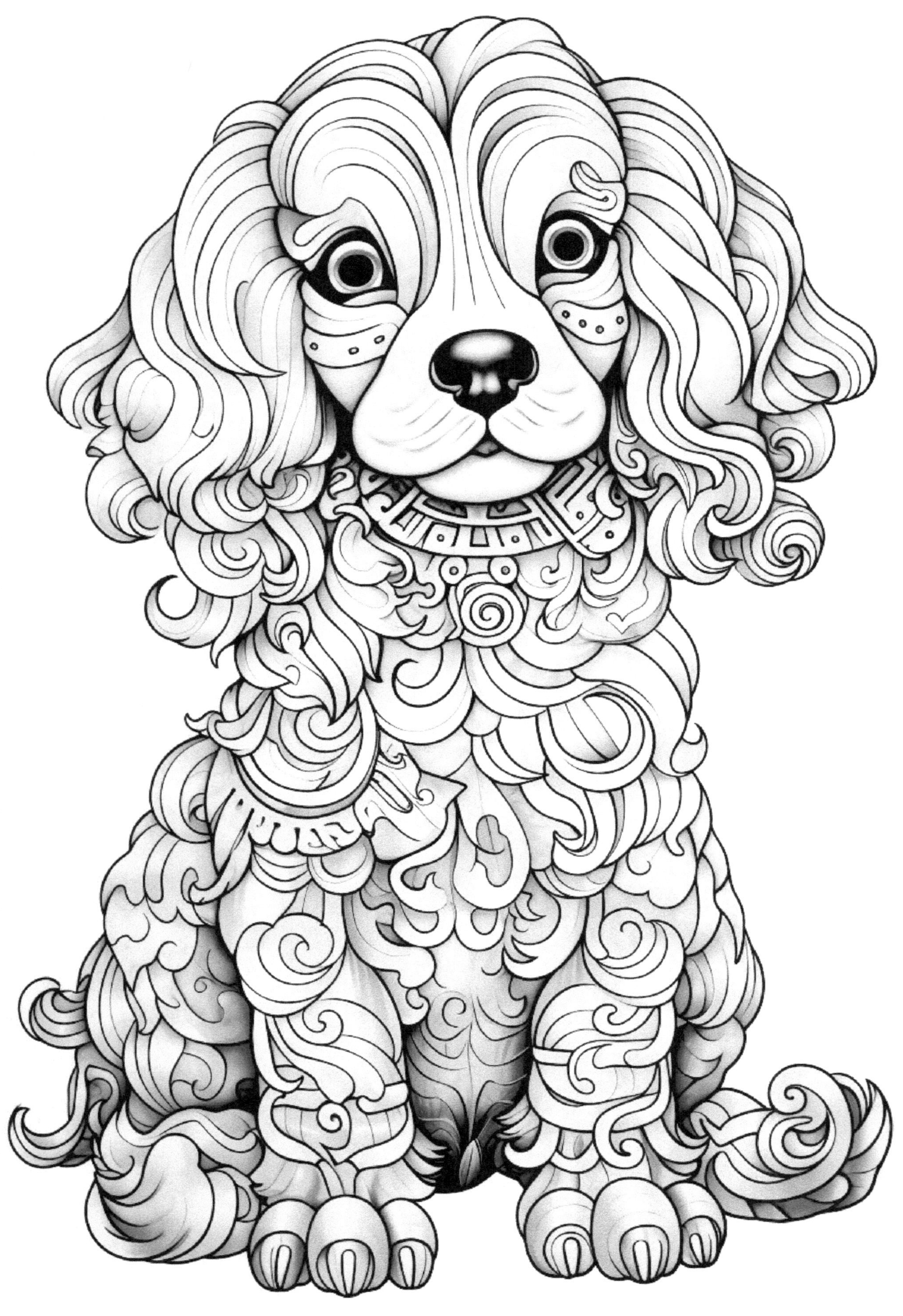

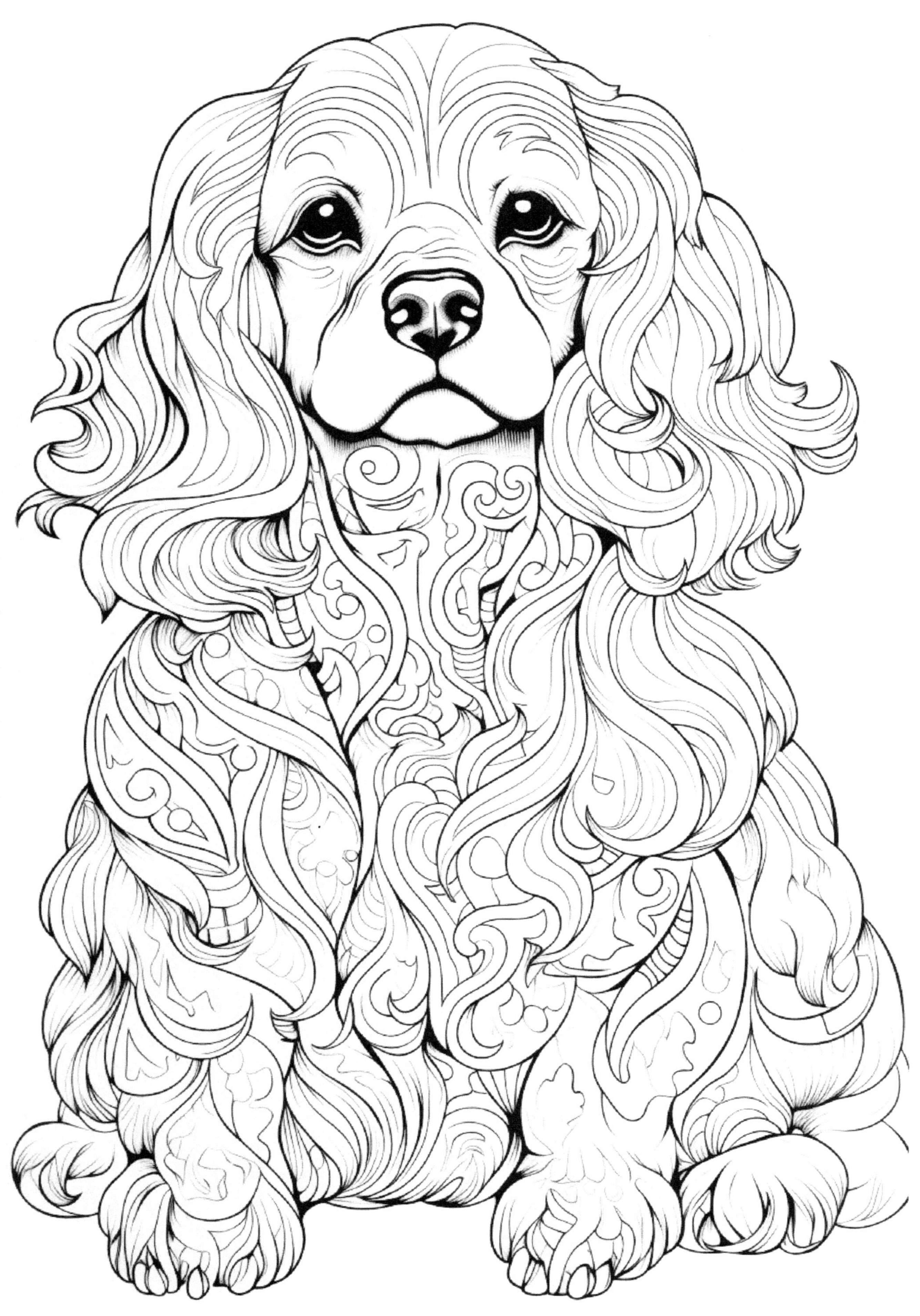

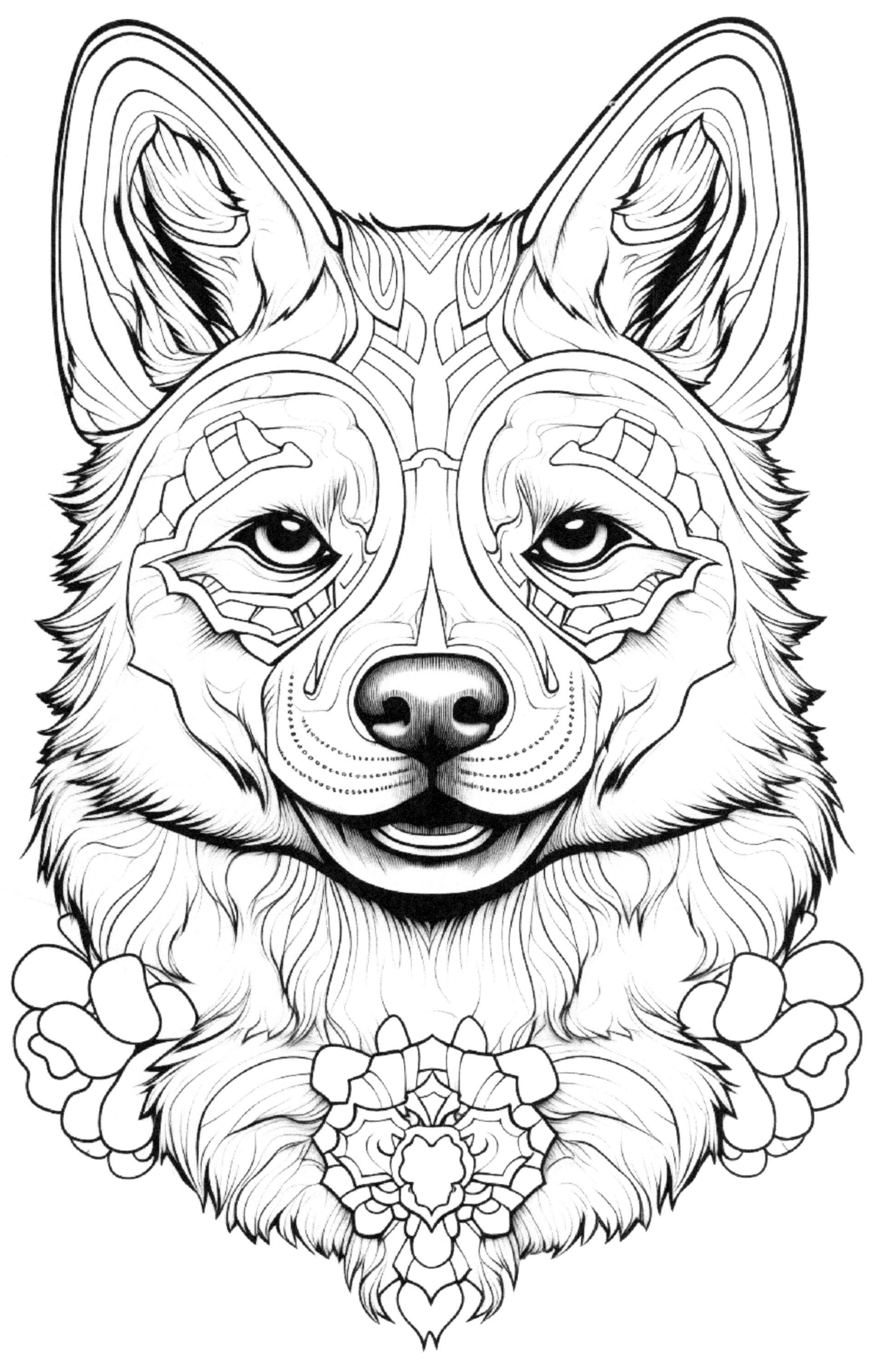

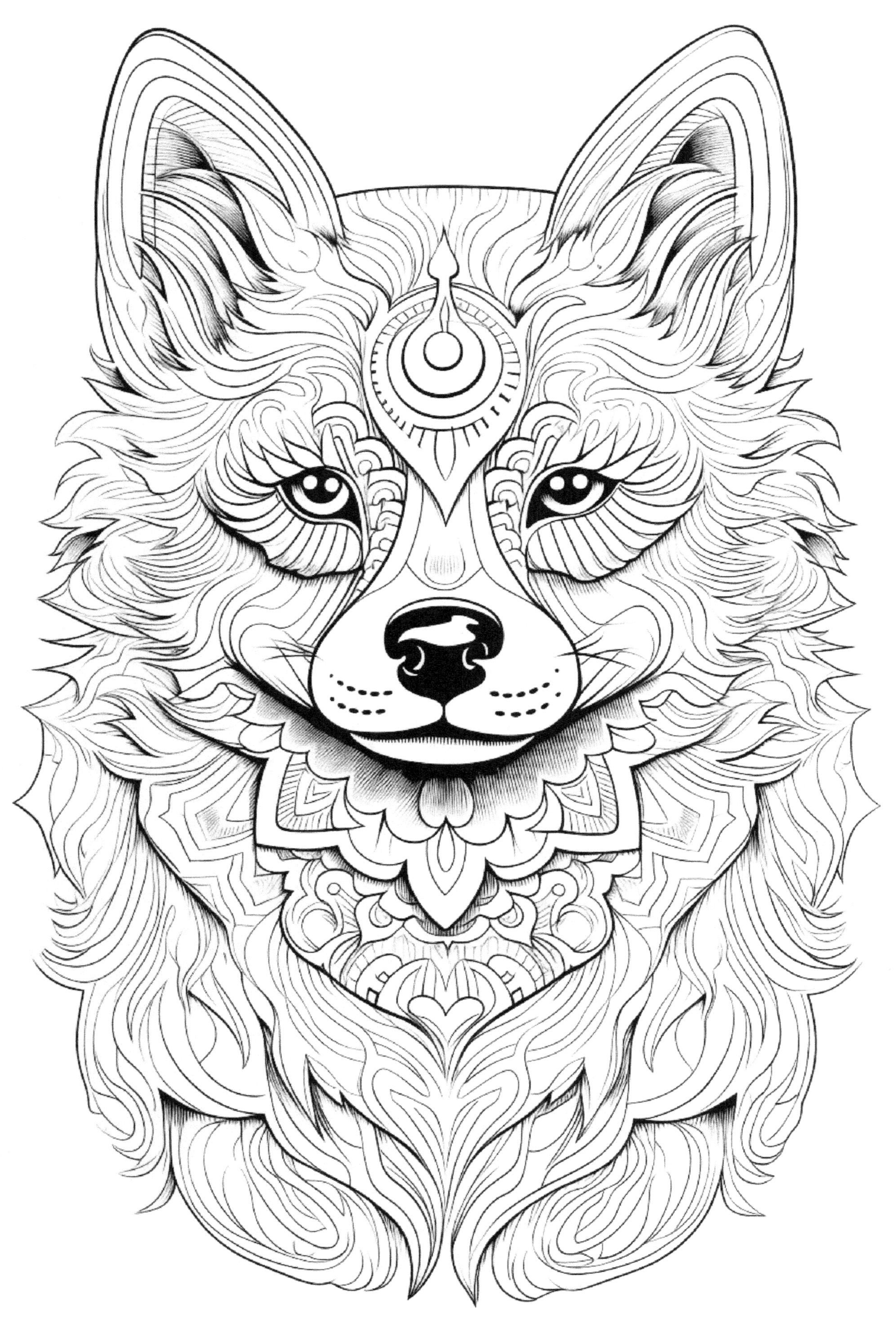

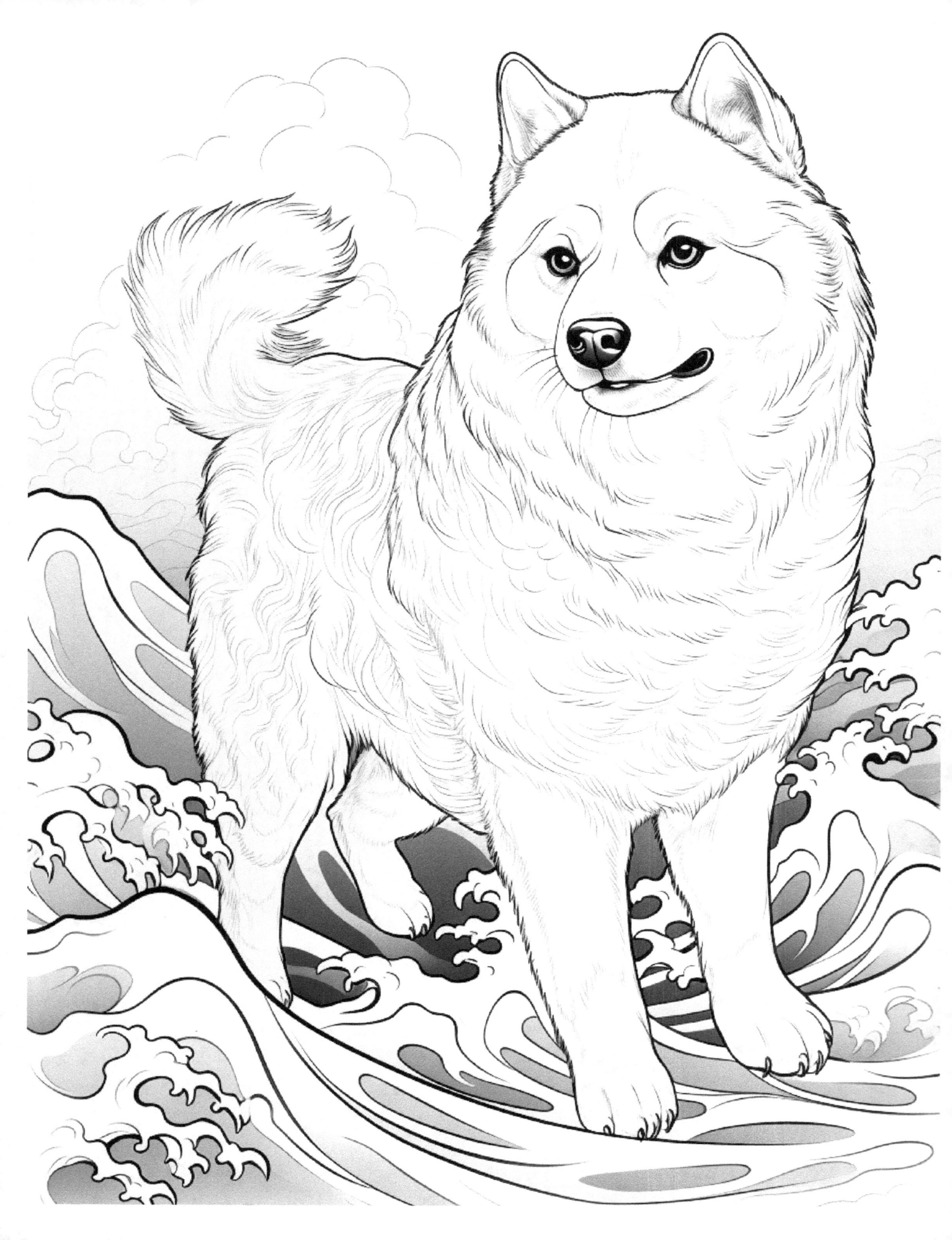

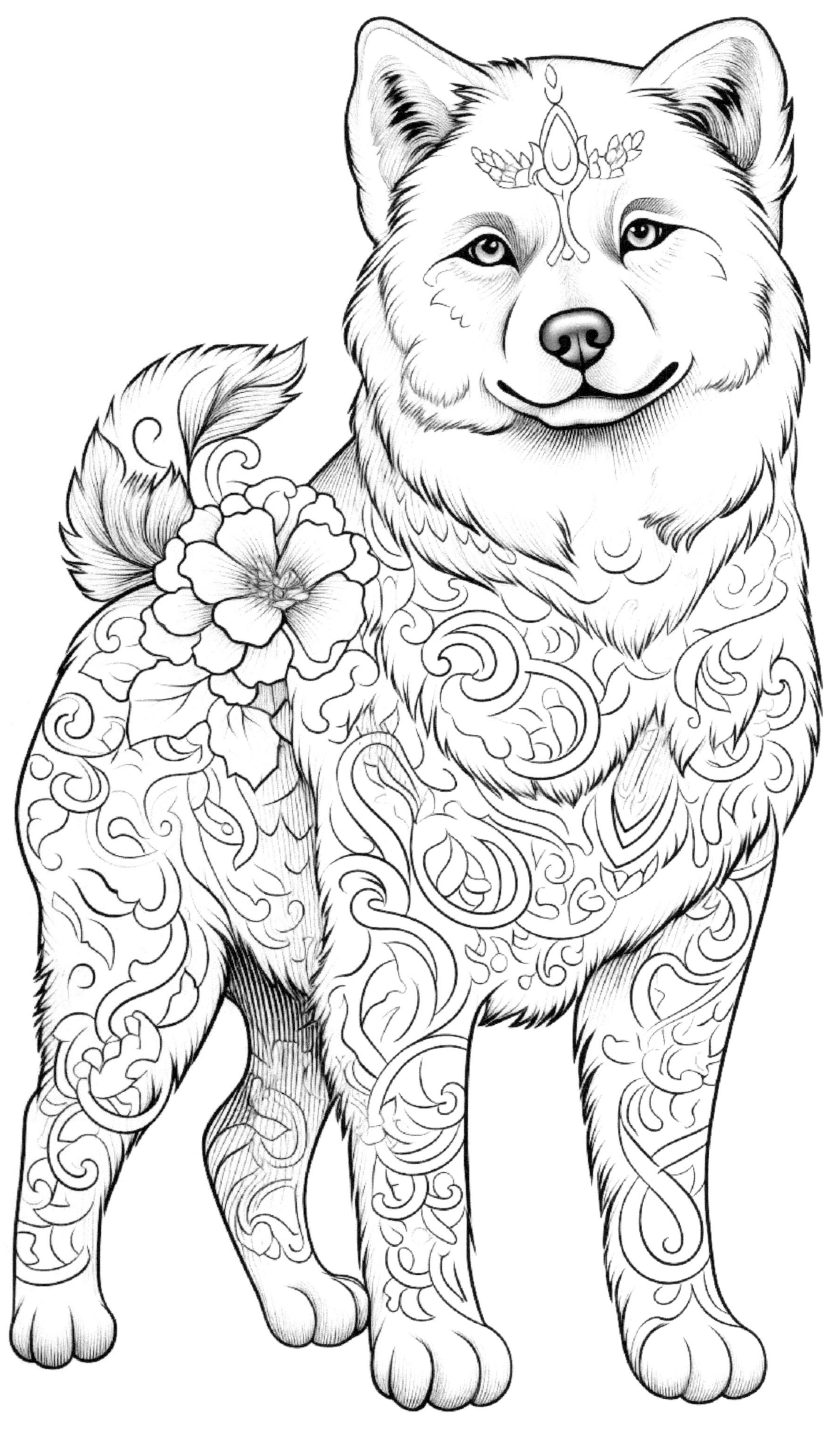

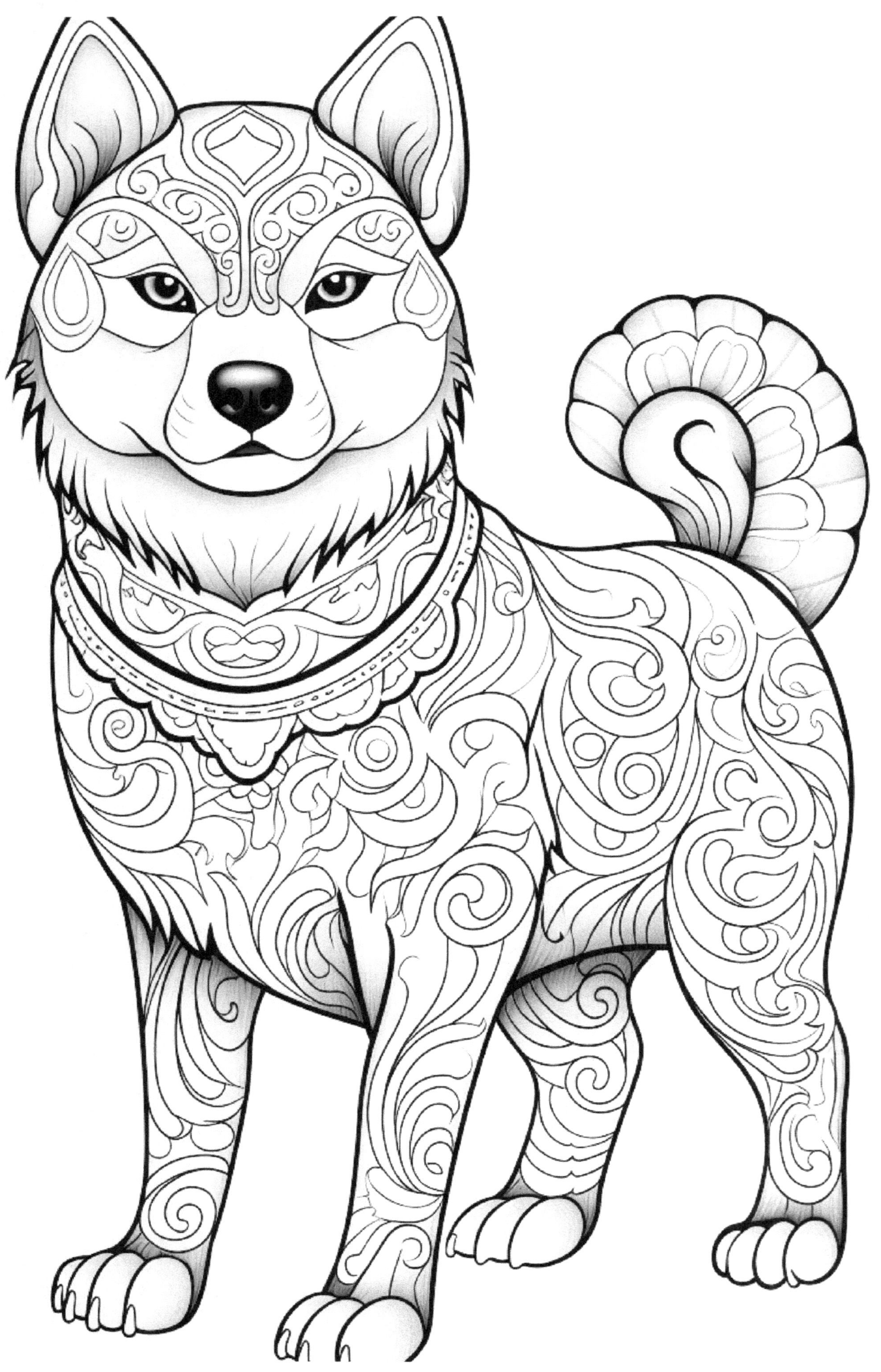

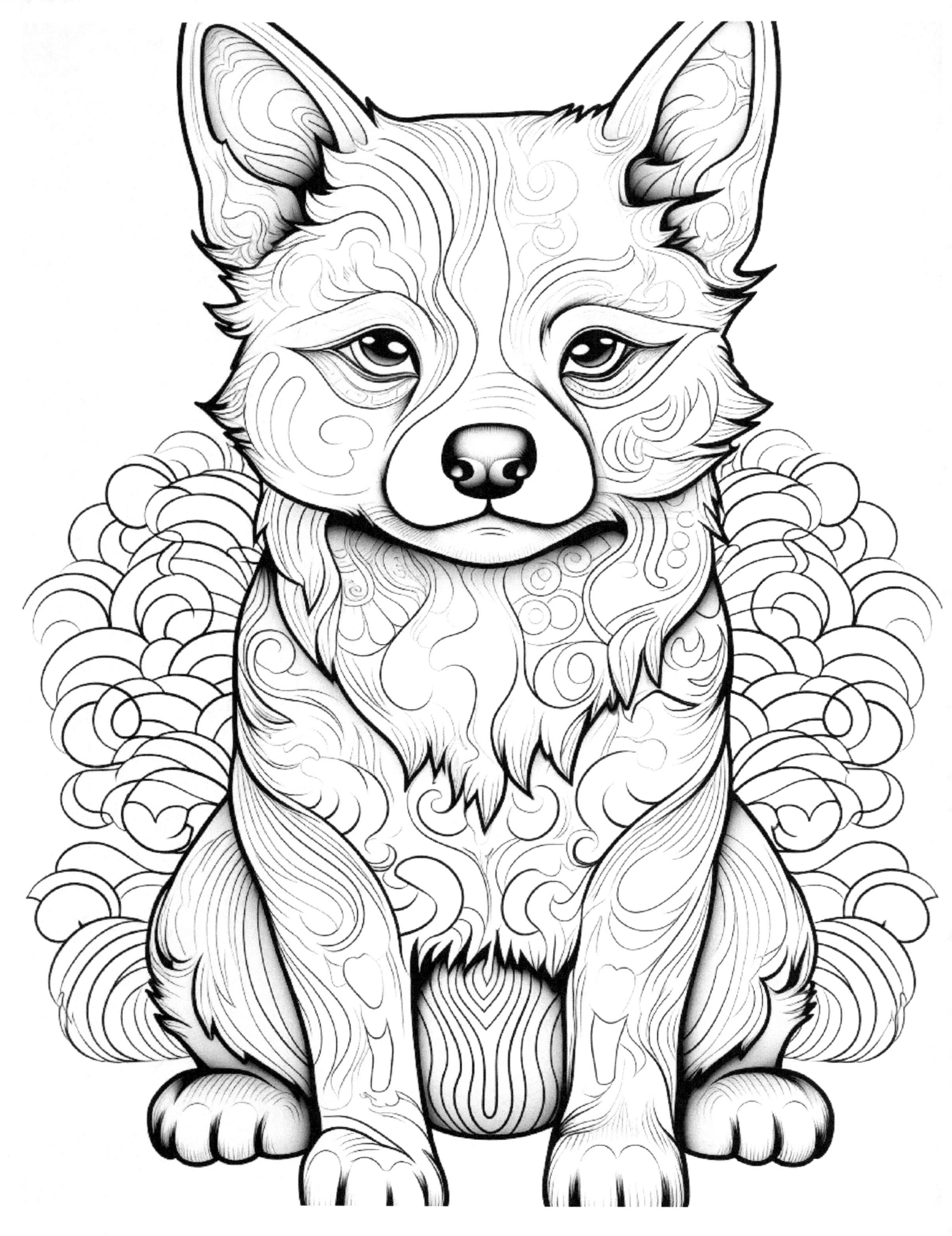

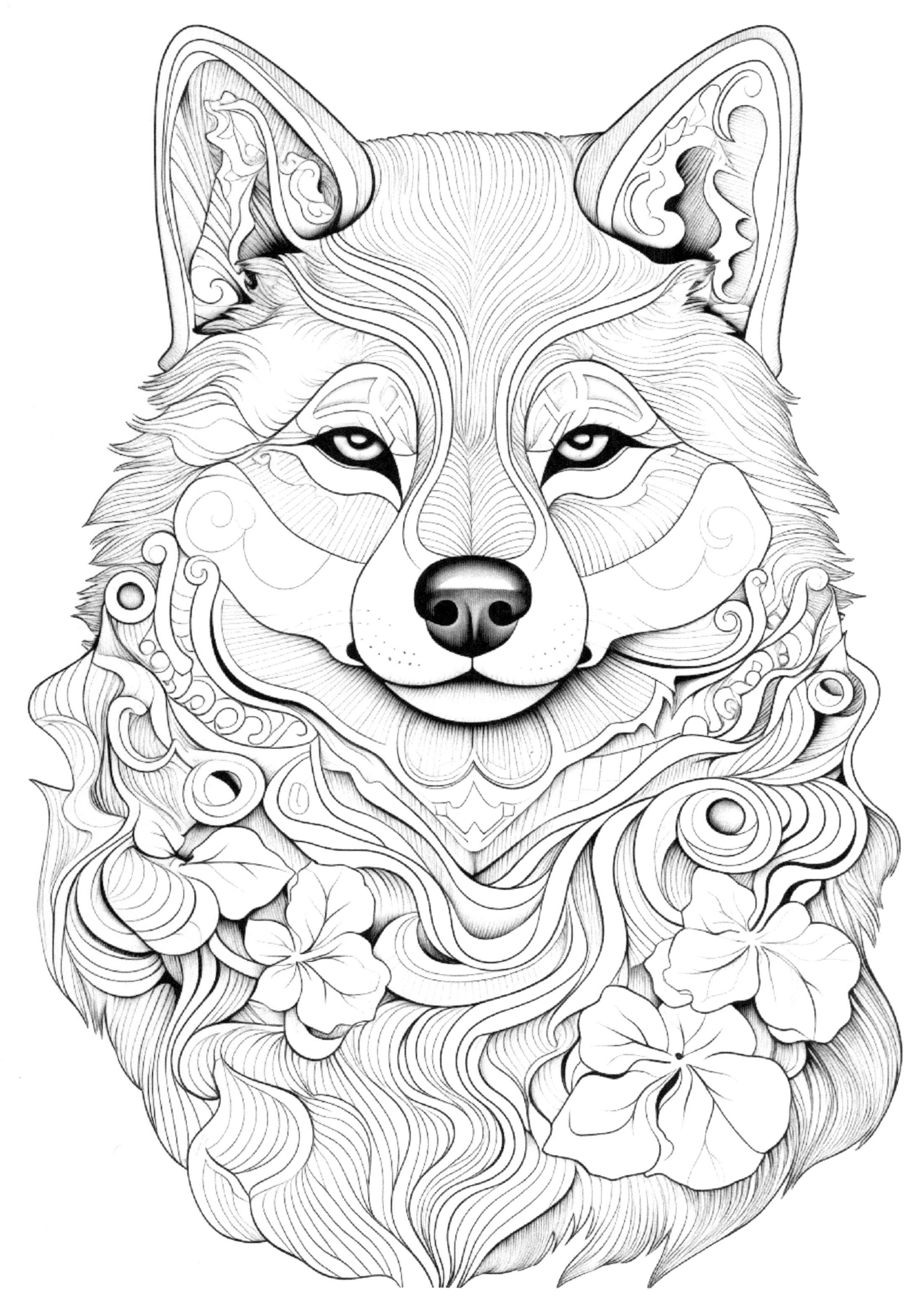

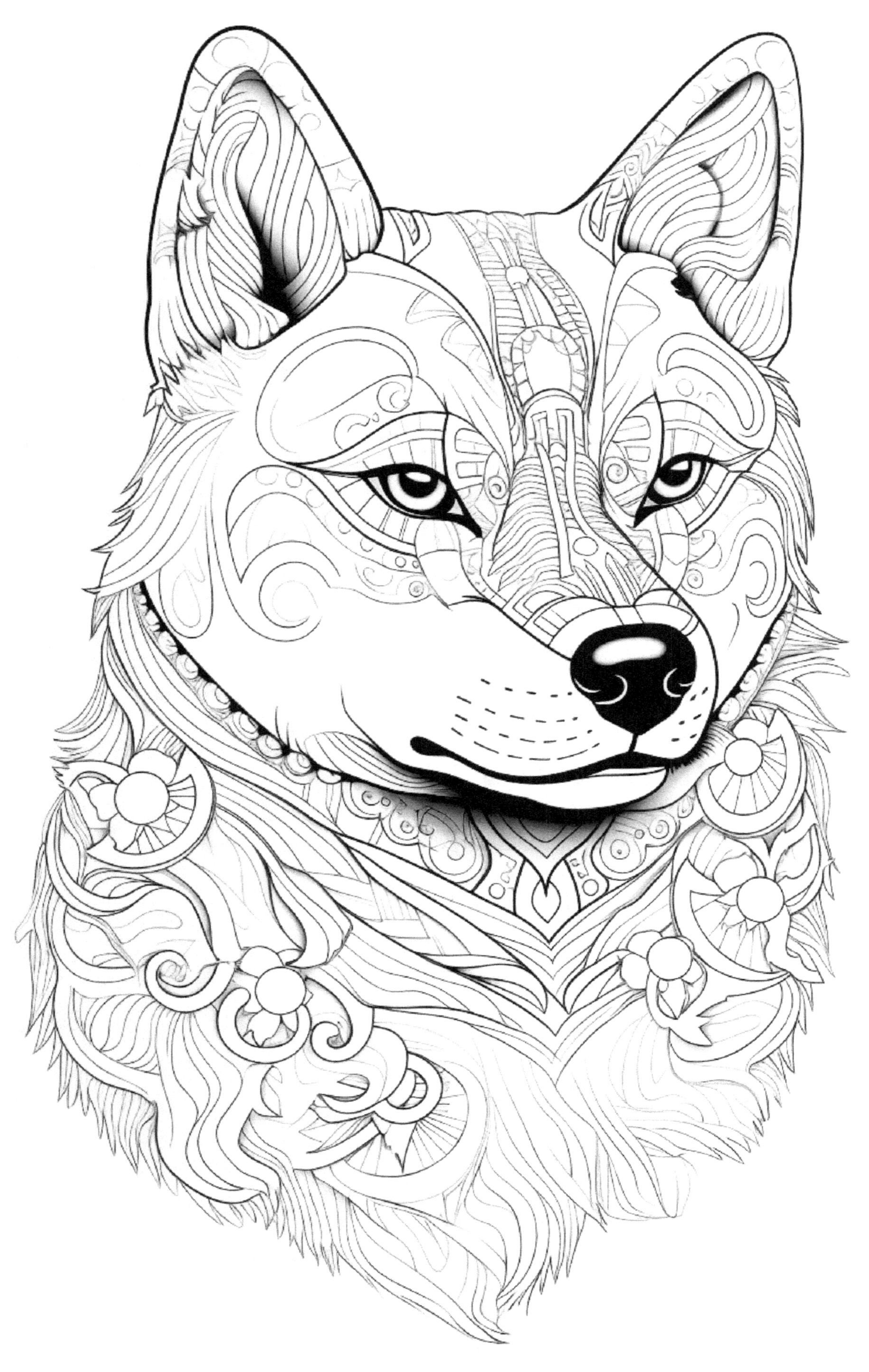

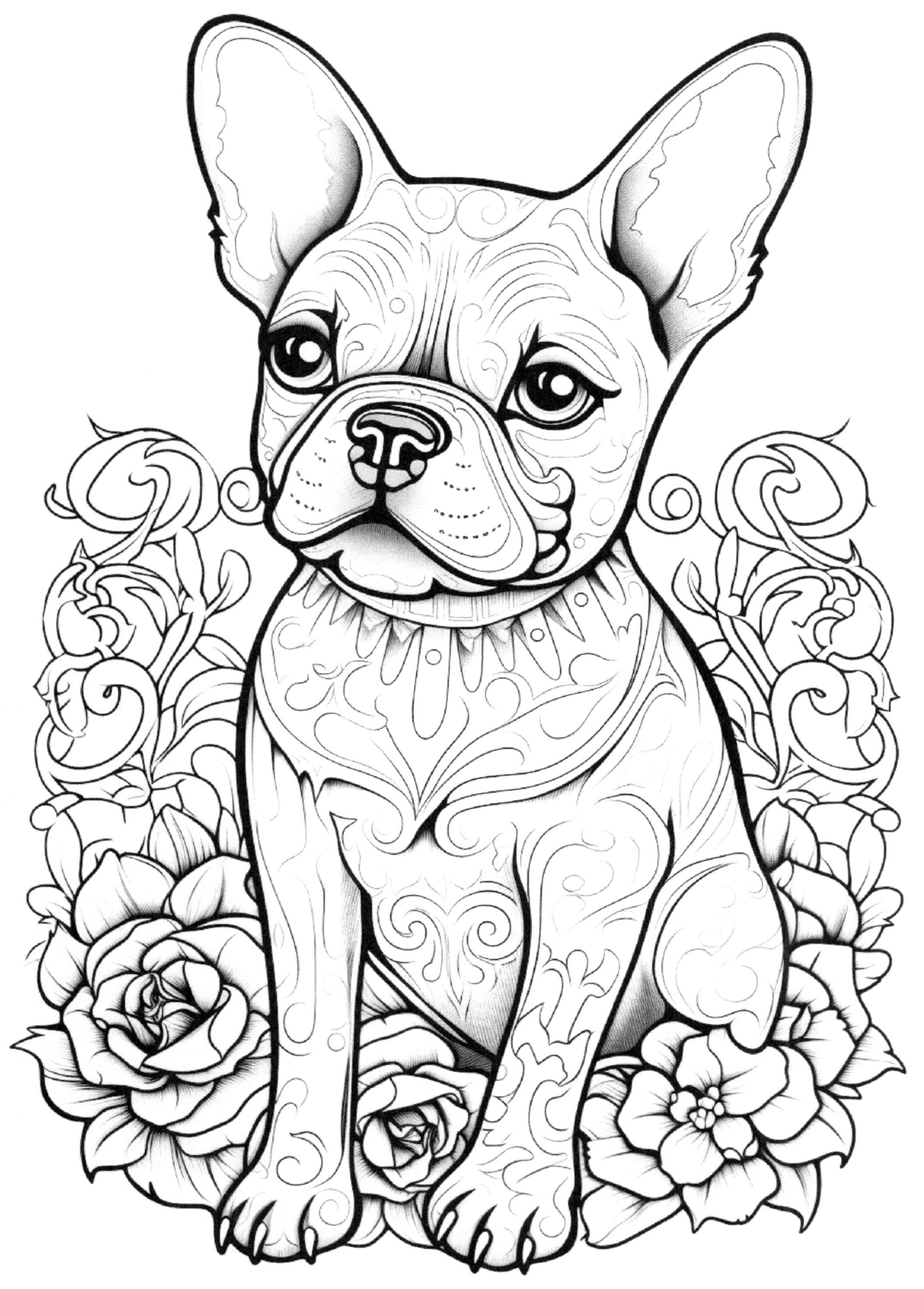

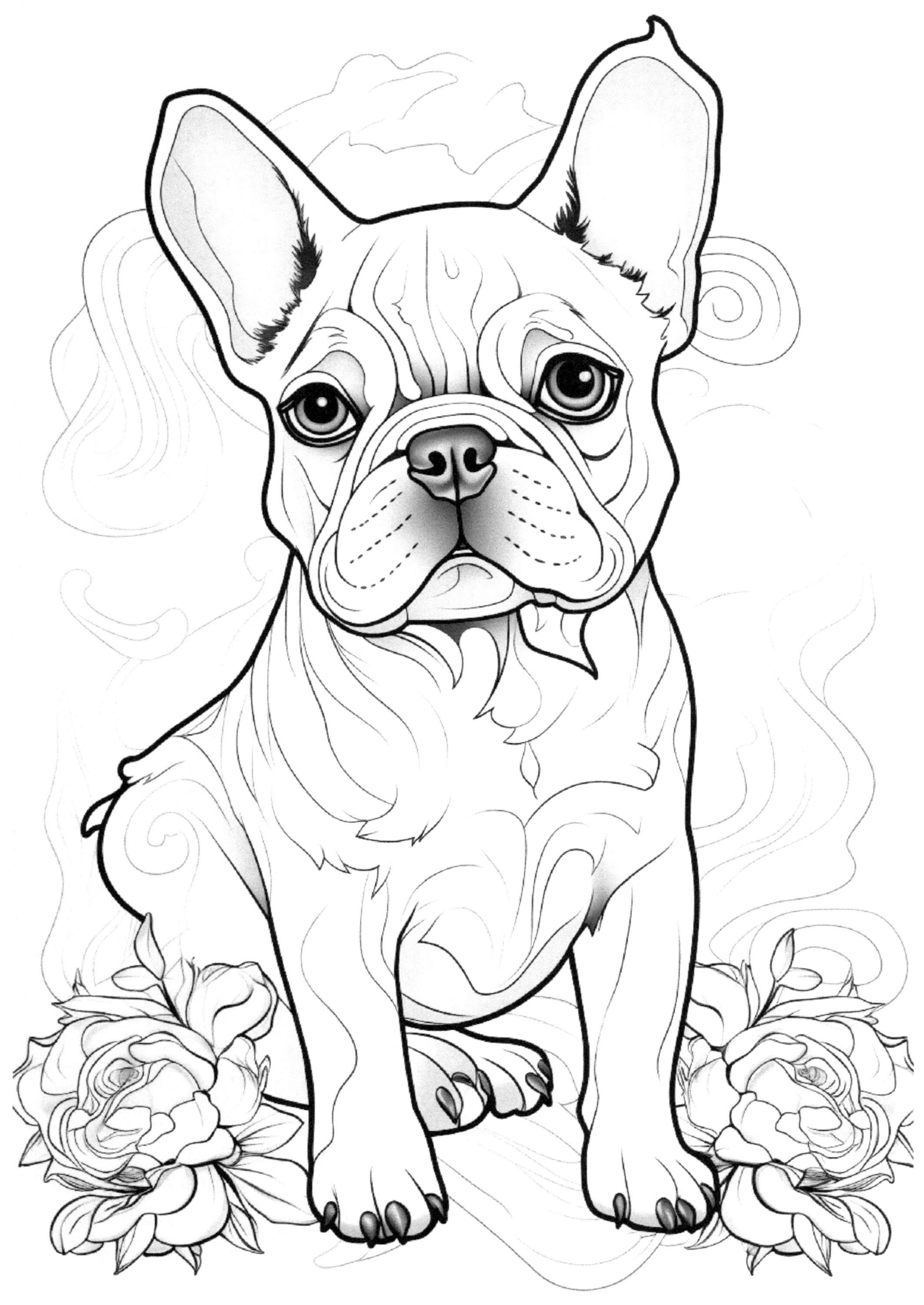

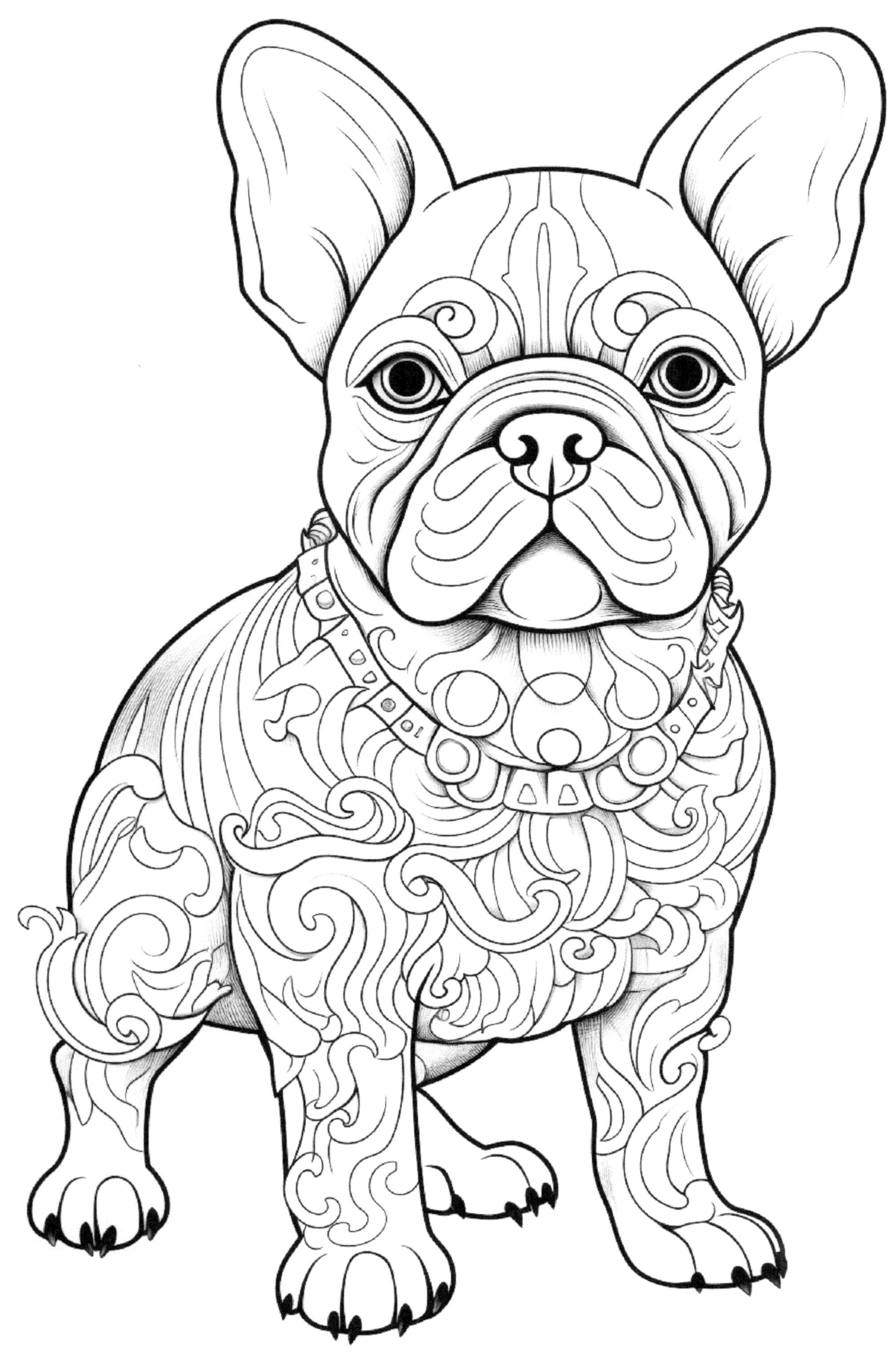

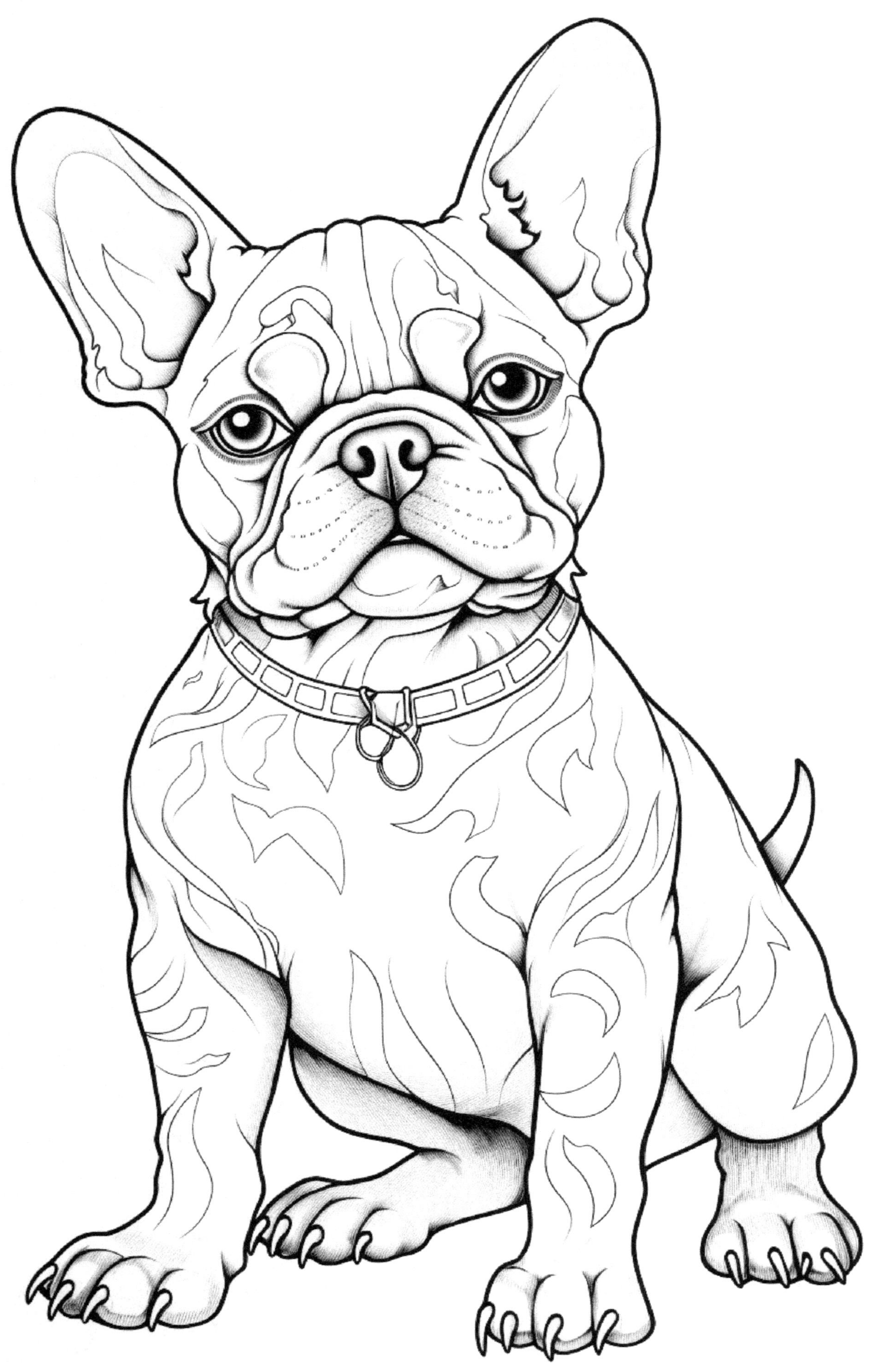

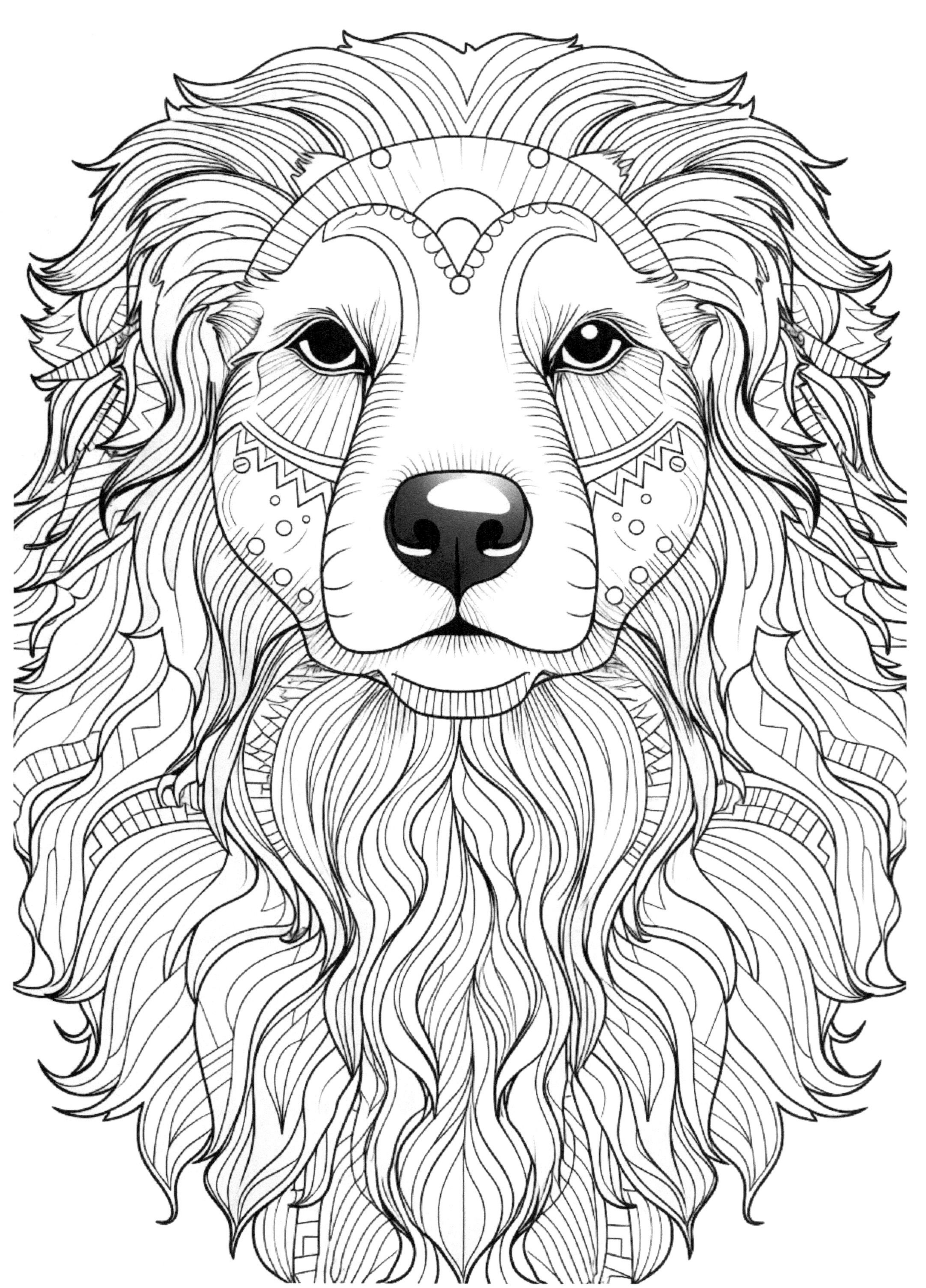

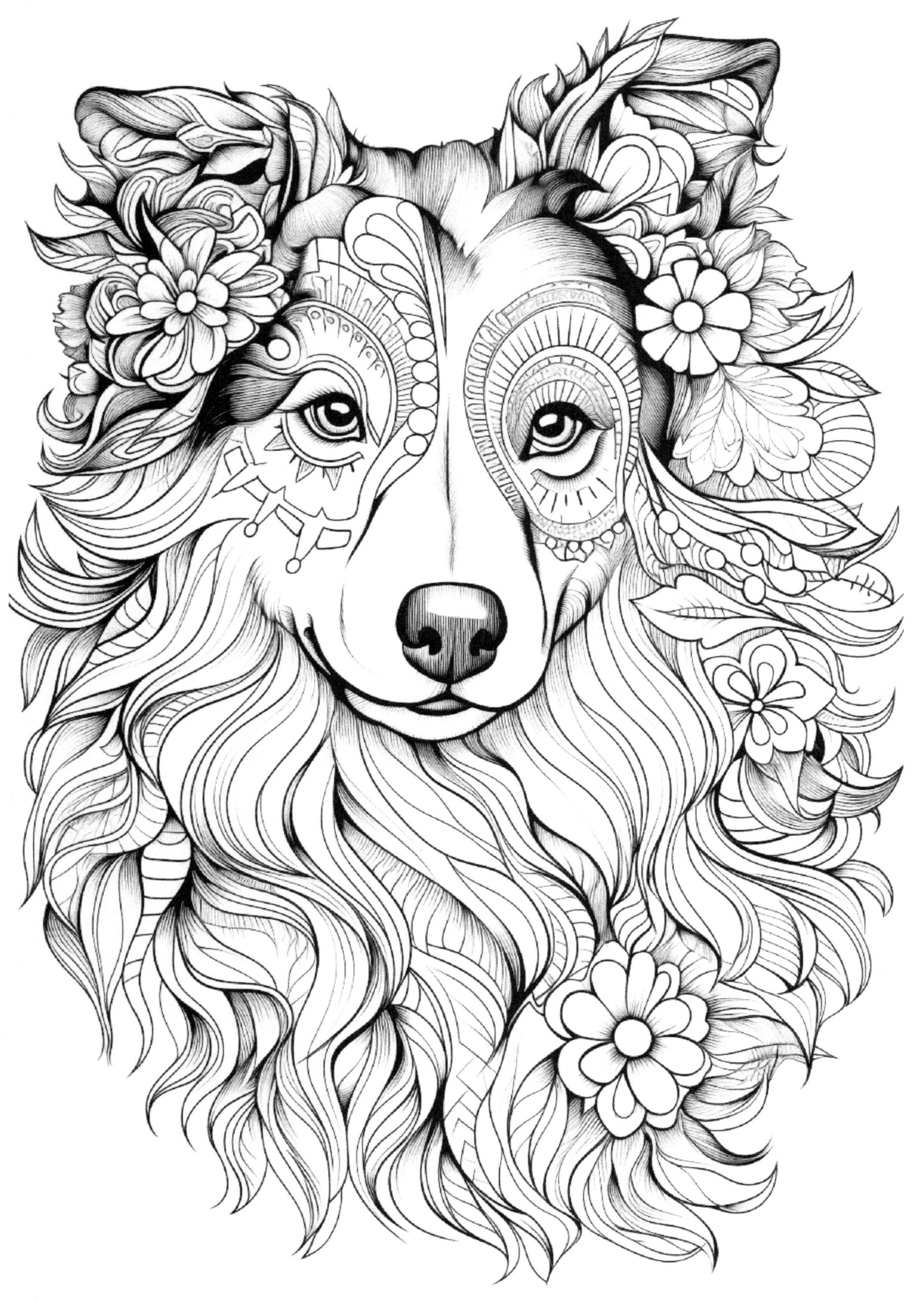

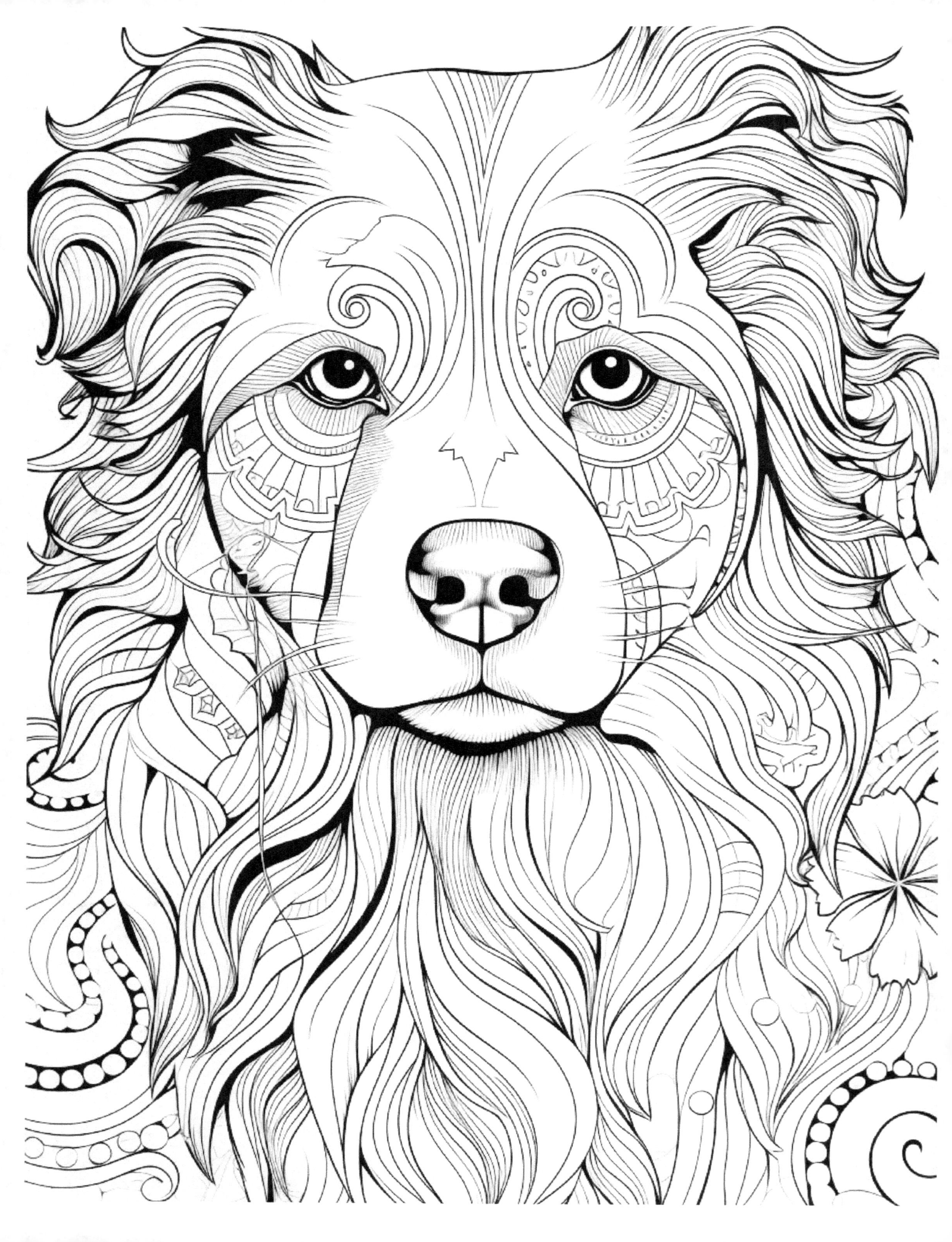

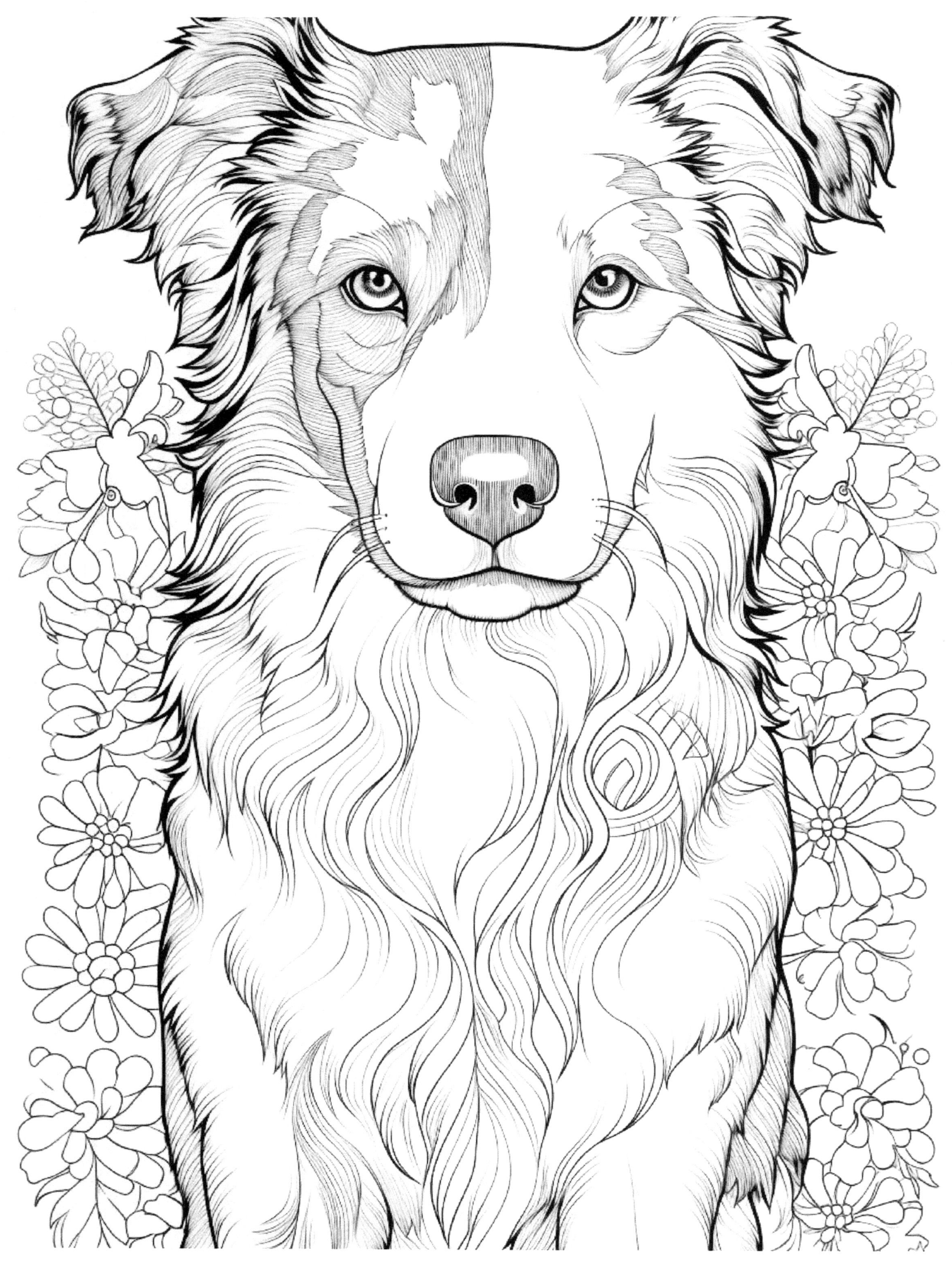

SPECIAL THANKS

In each color, you find a moment of serenity. This book is more than art; it's a creative haven where dogs inspire joy and color brightens the soul. May each colored page be a reminder of the beauty you bring to the world. Keep coloring your life with love and creativity. Dogs are here to brighten our days, and their colors to fill our journey. May this coloring experience bring peace and smiles with every brushstroke. Thank you for sharing this moment of joy with us.

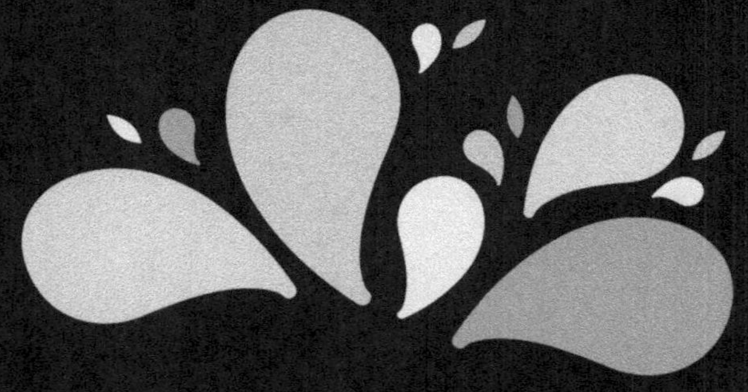

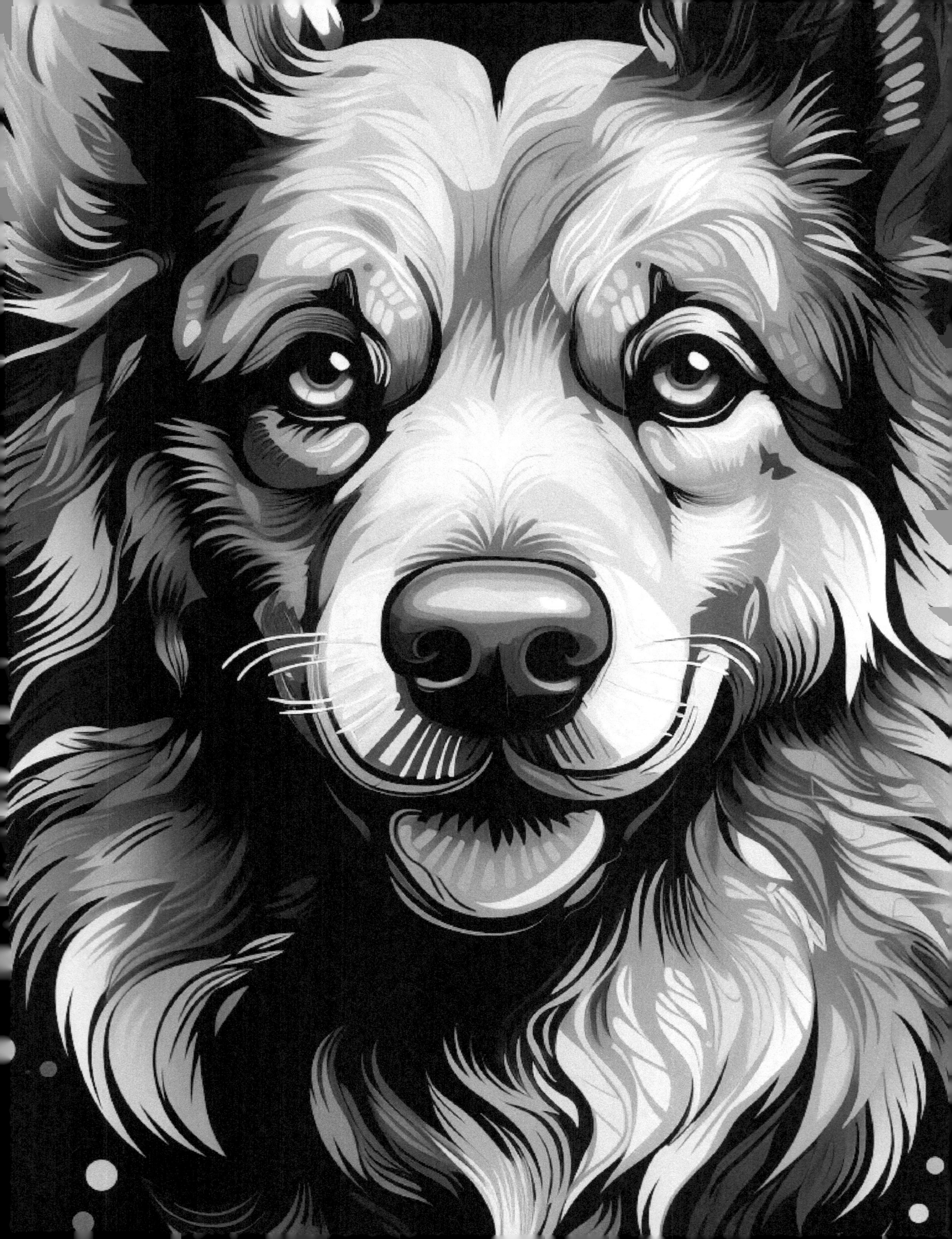